The Nature of Man

His World, His Spiritual Resources, His Destiny

The Nature of Man

His World · His Spiritual Resources · His Destiny

A DISCUSSION

by

LYNN HAROLD HOUGH

EDMUND W. SINNOTT

KIRTLEY F. MATHER

ORDWAY TEAD

BRAND BLANSHARD

MARY CECIL ALLEN

JOHN SUTHERLAND BONNELL

TARAKNATH DAS

GARDNER MURPHY

CORNELIUS KRUSÉ

LEWIS MUMFORD

Edited by A. WILLIAM LOOS
Assisted by LAWRENCE B. CHROW

Essay Index Reprint Series

BOOKS FOR LIBRARIES PRESS
FREEPORT, NEW YORK

STANDARD BOOK NUMBER:

8369-1042-7

LIBRARY OF CONGRESS CATALOG CARD NUMBER:

69-18930

PRINTED IN THE UNITED STATES OF AMERICA

Foreword

To DEEPEN our understanding of the nature of man is today of crucial importance. If we would diagnose with even a degree of accuracy the perilous times in which we live, we must sooner or later find an intelligible and satisfying answer to the question, "What is man?"

The perplexing paradoxes of our era, the century in which science is predominant, are legion. Science, with its manifold inventions, has unified mankind. It has demonstrated the abundant resources for a full life for all. It has devised communications that demolish barriers and make neighbors of all peoples. It has traced the common cultural design in all areas of the earth. Yet, in this same century, conflicts of demonic bitterness have bred between nationalities. Divisions within humanity have been intensified. Irrational and brutal forces have broken out with satanic malignancy. The rise into power of new closed societies appears to block the search for a one-world civilization. The century's midpoint finds man in moral and mental confusion, gripped by fear, enervated by a sense of helplessness.

A vast number of social and natural scientists, as well as moralists, religious leaders, and publicists agree that we can gain insight into our complex era only as we plumb more deeply the dynamics of human nature.

The fundamental purpose of this book is to show how science, philosophy, and religion contribute to an under-

v

standing of the nature of man. The various authors seek to interpret the interrelationship of these disciplines as each helps contemporary man to find a way out of his present serious global predicament. Finally, the book aims to indicate clearly that, however intricate our political and economic problems, the real crisis we now face is moral and spiritual and must be met on that plane.

In his introductory chapter, Dr. Lynn Harold Hough presents a synoptic view of the subject matter treated by the other authors, each a specialist in his own field. Dr. Edmund W. Sinnott and Dr. Kirtley F. Mather speak for the natural scientists, the former dealing specifically with the way in which man transcends the natural world of which he is a part, the latter describing some of the natural resources on which man can depend.

An educator, Dr. Ordway Tead, writes a general chapter on the contribution the social sciences can make to an understanding of the place, power, and purpose of man in the world today. Dr. Gardner Murphy, a psychologist, elucidates the interrelations of persons, the primitive fellow-feeling that draws people together, the merits of the democratic or cooperative process over the competitive one; at the same time he throws light on the ultimate destiny of man as viewed from the vantage point of psychic research.

Chapter 6 interprets the relation of human artistic expression to the whole man; although Miss Mary Cecil Allen writes only about painting, the principles she enunciates can also be applied to literature, sculpture, and other forms of art.

Dr. Brand Blanshard deals with some of the ills that afflict man's inner life and suggests how the new techniques of psychotherapy can help to heal man and make him whole again. Two chapters deal with religious disciplines, the one by Dr. John S. Bonnell written from the point of view of the West, the other by Dr. Taraknath Das from the standpoint of the East.

Although the perspective of this entire book embraces the one-world idea, Dr. Cornelius Krusé deals specifically with ways in which "the world man" can be developed and the manner in which philosophy can contribute to this quest. Finally, Dr. Lewis Mumford in a concluding chapter has written a summary and synthesis of the entire series.

No attempt was made in this series to obtain a unified point of view, except that all participants sought to contribute to an understanding of our era by focusing attention upon the nature of man. Each author, therefore, assumes full responsibility for interpretations and opinions in his own presentation.

The material in this symposium, with the exception of two chapters, was delivered in a series of lectures in New York City during 1949. The lectures were so well received that we were urged to print them and make them available to a larger audience.

One reason for printing this book is that we hope leaders in other communities may arrange a similar lecture series. In Appendix B we have outlined in detail how the series was arranged in the hope that these data might prove suggestive to others when planning similar programs.

It is not possible in a limited space to express our appreciation to the many individuals who have contributed to the success of the lecture series and to the publishing of this volume. Our debt of gratitude is deep to each of the recognized leaders in their respective fields who contributed to this symposium, and also to the other leaders who actively participated in the lecture series as chairmen or in other ways. Dr. Walter D. Head, President of the World Alliance, and Mr. John R. Inman, Assistant Secretary of The Church Peace Union, gave valuable help in arranging the lecture series. Dr. A. William Loos, assisted by Mr. Lawrence B. Chrow, edited the manuscript.

To Mrs. Ruth Cranston we express our special thanks. The

idea of this series originated with her, and she was in large measure responsible for organizing the symposium and securing the lecturers.

HENRY A. ATKINSON
General Secretary
The Church Peace Union

Merrill House
170 East 64th Street
New York 21, New York
January, 1950

Contents

Contributors

LYNN HAROLD HOUGH
Clergyman, Educator and Author

EDMUND W. SINNOTT
Chairman, Department of Botany, Yale University
Director, Sheffield Scientific School, Yale University

KIRTLEY F. MATHER
Professor of Geology, Harvard University

ORDWAY TEAD
Chairman, Board of Higher Education, New York City

BRAND BLANSHARD
Professor of Philosophy, Yale University

MARY CECIL ALLEN
Artist and Author

JOHN SUTHERLAND BONNELL
Minister, The Fifth Avenue Presbyterian Church, New York City

TARAKNATH DAS
Professor of Public Affairs, New York University
Lecturer in History and World Politics, Columbia University

GARDNER MURPHY
Professor of Psychology at The City College of New York
Lecturer in Psychology at Columbia University

CORNELIUS KRUSÉ
Professor of Philosophy, Wesleyan University, Middletown, Connecticut
Chairman, American Council of Learned Societies

LEWIS MUMFORD
Author and Lecturer

The Nature of Man

His World, His Spiritual Resources, His Destiny

1

Introduction: The Dignity of Man

LYNN HAROLD HOUGH

IN ONE of the most brilliant and provocative paragraphs of
Arnold J. Toynbee's monumental work, *A Study of History,*
we find these sentences: "Why should we suppose that the
scientific method of thought—a method which has been devised for thinking about Inanimate Nature—should be ap-
plicable to historical thought, which is a study of living
creatures and indeed of human beings? . . . We are sufficiently on our guard against the so-called 'Pathetic Fallacy' of
imaginatively endowing inanimate objects with life. We
now fall victims to the inverse 'Apathetic Fallacy' of treating
living creatures as though they were inanimate."[1]

The following chapters deal with human beings, their
characteristics, their place in the world, and the possibilities
of their life together. Each writer speaks from the standpoint
of a particular discipline which he has pursued with devoted
concentration and with distinguished success. There is no
attempt to secure formal or artificial agreement. In fact, dis-
agreements appear throughout the book. All the more remarkable are the areas of agreement, and all the more im-
pressive is the common witness as to the dignity of man and
the lofty possibilities of human life. If there sometimes appears a tendency to extend the range of a particular approach
so that it becomes a complete philosophy of life, one sees at

---

[1] Vol. I, pp. 7-8. Oxford University Press, New York, 1934.

once how natural this is in an age of specialists. It is more important that a synoptic view will include something of far reaching significance from each of the departments of thought represented in this book.

Once and again in these chapters there is an attack upon materialism. Once and again there is a repudiation of a mechanistic interpretation of human life. Once and again there is an emphasis upon purpose. And there is a constant sense of those values which must be accepted and preserved in the very name of a good life for men. Here you have a group of earnest men of great good will, each with adequate competence in his own field, setting about to see the significance of that in man which gives solid basis for high hopes for his future.

MAN THE CONTROLLER

The fashion in which all these insights can be integrated and made a part of a corpus of thought about man which will release all human powers for triumphant achievement is shown in that Christian humanism which has had so long and so distinguished a history and which has revealed so happy a capacity to receive truth from every source and to see the whole of life in the light of its own deep and abiding insights.

Man the controller stands out in sharp clarity in this type of thought. And each chapter of this book in its own way bears witness to the centrality of this position. The biologist is an example of the work of the human mind mastering and controlling vast and important materials. The earth is surveyed in such fashion as to see how man can best control and make permanent its multiplied and varied products. The social sciences see man accepting thoughts and entering upon courses of action which will develop and will conserve the good life. The subconscious is inspected by man's controlling intelligence which seeks and finds methods for its wise utilization. Art sees man controlling and using material forms so as to secure an authentic experience of beauty. The man of prayer controls his thought to turn his attention toward God. And the man who uses the methods of Indian religious discipline studies their ways, estimates their possibilities and chooses among them. The man who sets out to show how psychical research itself brings forth much knowledge which shows men's interdependence and the possibilities of their cooperation is himself investigating large bodies of material and so perceiving their meaning and turning them to such purpose as to further the human cause. The interpreter who reveals philosophy busy about universal human values and showing the way to a mutual and world-wide understanding is controlling and using his intelligence to great purpose. The synthetic thinker who shows man in process of making the most of his possibilities through the achievement of an integrated self in a world of integrated selves is using his intelligence as he works at this high enterprise. Man the controller appears everywhere. And so we begin to see the significance of the distinctive quality of man.

THE POSITION OF CHRISTIAN HUMANISM

All of this the Christian humanist gladly welcomes and fits onto his own corpus of thought. He sees man over nature under God. He sees man using his intelligence to choose among alternatives freely chosen after the closest and the most critical investigation. He sees man's profoundest kinships not with the mathematical order in which he finds himself and in respect of which he has achieved such remarkable control but in connection with the supremacy of moral and spiritual values; and he turns to their classical expression in the Old Testament and the New, while he welcomes every evidence of the wide shining of the light which lighteth every man coming into the world. If he is an evangelical Christian, he will see the very expression of the deepest meaning of human life in the life and teaching of Jesus Christ. And he finds his profoundest contact with what he firmly believes to be eternal reality in the cross of Christ with its expression of the suffering love of God. He does not live in one world as a thinker using his intelligence to understand and in another turning his emotions and his will to moral and spiritual and social values. He uses all of his powers in each of his experiences and finds in the sanctions of religion the fulfilment of the deepest outreaches of every aspect of his life.

The Christian cannot accept the assertion that the very structure of man's life is essentially evil. He knows the tragedy of the misuse of human freedom. He also knows that God made man for the good use of freedom. And he knows that only by a good use of freedom does man answer to God's purpose in his creation.

The Christian knows when he follows the true humanistic tradition that men were made for a good life together. Men were made for fellowship. They were not made for antagonism. And in the deepest experience of religion man meets God and receives an inner peace in whose profound potencies there is good promise as men accept them for the peace of mankind.

SUGGESTIONS FOR FURTHER READING

Louis J. H. Mercier. *American Humanism and the New Age.* Milwaukee: Bruce Publishing Company, 1948.

Lynn Harold Hough. *The Meaning of Human Experience.* New York: Abingdon-Cokesbury, 1945.

Lynn Harold Hough. *Christian Humanism and the Modern World.* Toronto: The Ryerson Press, 1949.

Dr. Lynn Harold Hough has been described by Principal R. C. Wallace of Queens University as "an outstanding exponent of Christian humanism in our times." For many years he was dean of Drew Theological Seminary and a member of the Executive Committee of the Federal Council of Churches of Christ in America. He has been pastor

*of outstanding churches in the United States and summer preacher on
many occasions at such British churches as the City Temple in London
and Wellington Church in Glasgow. He is the author of over forty
books. Two of them,* The Christian Criticism of Life *and* The Meaning
of Human Experience, *have been Religious Book Club selections.*

2

Man's Place in Nature as Seen by a Biologist

EDMUND W. SINNOTT

WHATEVER else a man may be, we should never forget that he is an animal.

An important part of his nature is involved in this fact. Evolution, the great idea of the nineteenth century, made it clear that the whole world of living things is related and has been developed from the very simple beginnings of life. Man has his place in the animal kingdom. He belongs to the great group of vertebrate animals and to the highest class in it, the mammals. Among the mammals he is a primate and stands at the top of this series.

Since all living things belong to the same great family, he is brother to all creatures. This is a very different idea of man from that which prevailed a century ago. Whether we are to regard him as a fallen angel or a risen ape is an important problem.

MAN A PHYSICO-CHEMICAL ORGANISM

As a living thing man shares with all others certain characteristics. The basis of his life is in protoplasm. This is now being actively studied by all the biological disciplines, including biophysics and biochemistry. Protoplasm is composed of proteins. It has specific chemical qualities. It is sensitive. It is reproductive. It possesses the remarkable capacity to build the organized systems which we call organisms.

The physiological study of man, thus based on our knowl-

7

edge of living substance, has yielded much information about him. Medicine has learned to manipulate man's biological constitution in many ways. He can be modified by diet and drugs. His whole personality may be changed by severing the frontal lobes of his brain. In one important sense man is, therefore, a physico-chemical system.

MECHANISM OR PURPOSEFUL BEING?

Man is thus not only a brother to all living things, but a brother to the dust as well. This is a sobering thought and introduces other questions about him. Is he simply a machine? If so, what happens to freedom, purpose and responsibility? This is a major philosophical problem. Much authority from biology is ranged on the side of a mechanistic explanation. This is the only way that science can study physiology. Against this point of view stands the verdict of common sense, the vivid conviction that we are free and masters of our own fates. To maintain anything else would, as Professor Jennings[1] suggests, demand too great a sacrifice of common sense to logic. Even on the side of physiology the mechanists have as yet not solved their problem, for there are many unanswered questions that the scientist must face. The whole question of the mechanistic interpretation of human life is too vast for us to solve here, but we should not underestimate its seriousness. Whatever our decisions in these matters may be, for all practical purposes we must treat man as if he were a free and purposeful creature. He is certainly a very different animal from any other and his tremendous advance shows the vast possibilities inherent in protoplasm. Life can produce a Shakespeare and a Beethoven.

MAN TRANSCENDS THE ANIMAL WORLD

Man is higher than the beasts in various ways. He is far

---

[1] See Herbert S. Jennings, *The Universe and Life,* New Haven, Yale University Press, 1933. In this connection Professor Jennings refers to Bergson's *Creative Evolution.*

more intelligent. He has the ability to control nature through the enormous advances in science. This has developed in him an intellectual view of the world and its problems.

He is educable. With man comes a new type of progress, mental and not merely biological. Here we can speak of social rather than physical inheritance. Man can gather up the past and move rapidly ahead without waiting for the slow process of evolutionary advance.

He is a social being. As such he is faced with the whole problem of living with his fellows and developing a morality. This is very vital today when a most important question is whether our ethical sense can keep pace with our intellectual progress.

THE HUMAN SPIRIT SEEKS VALUES

All this is getting further away from man as a machine. There is one other capacity of greatest significance that he has. He is a sensitive instrument for the perception of qualities in the universe impossible of access to the intellect alone. He is moved by beauty in all its forms. He aspires to virtue. He seeks a glimpse of the great mystery of the universe. Here, in what we call the human spirit, are manifest the highest possibilities inherent in protoplasm.

Does this enable man to look more deeply into the universe than he can by his mind alone? To many, such an idea seems pure illusion. To them, mysticism is a hateful word. Here again we face a deep problem that has troubled man from the beginning. We cannot solve it now, but tough-minded intellectualism and scorn of the way of the spirit are by no means the view of all philosophers and scientists, as Professor C. E. M. Joad, Sir Arthur Eddington, Herbert J. Muller, William James, Joseph Needham, and many others bear eloquent witness. In this connection Needham[2] says: "If it is the activity of the human spirit that brings it specially into touch with the central point of the universe, we

---

[2] *The Skeptical Biologist*, p. 40, New York, W. W. Norton & Co., 1930.

might find a worse metaphor than that of resonance, conceiving of philosophy and of science and of poetry, also, as nothing more than a hum given forth by the bronze bell of man as it catches a note from the eternal harmony and thrills respondingly from base to rim."

THE SPIRITUAL ANSWER TO THE MATERIALISTS

This is our problem: What is this protoplasmic system which we are?

There are two answers to our question. The first is suggested by a quotation from Bertrand Russell:[3] "That man is the product of causes which had no prevision of the end they were achieving; that his origin, his growth, his hopes and fears, his loves and beliefs, are but the outcome of accidental collocations of atoms. . . . all these things, if not quite beyond dispute, are yet so nearly certain, that no philosophy which rejects them can hope to stand." This gives a sweeping concept of man as a creature of the dust, bound by his environment, doomed to ultimate extinction, but struggling upward to the highest goals which he can know in a universe that is godless, purposeless and ultimately lifeless. This is the answer given by scientific humanism, by the tough-minded in all fields, by those who strive to reconcile the quantitative, materialistic philosophy of the sciences with man's sense of the imponderable values of which we have spoken.

The second answer is quite perfectly expressed in the Biblical quotation: "Thou has made him (man) a little lower than the angels and crowned him with glory and honor."[4] This is the answer given by a host of saints and seers and poets and philosophers of the past. It is the answer given today by those who believe that the intellect is not our only means of access to the truth and that man, brother

---

[3] "A Free Man's Worship" in *Mysticism and Logic*, pp. 47-8, New York, W. W. Norton & Co., 1929.

[4] Psalm 8.

though he may be to the dust and to the brutes, can reach across the chasm from the seen to the unseen and may become a citizen of the Kingdom of Heaven.

This great problem is, in the last analysis, a problem of life, a biological problem. Man is the noblest of animals, but what he really is, we do not know, nor shall we for a long time to come. But the answer to this question is of the utmost significance in an approach to those problems which confront mankind today.

SUGGESTIONS FOR FURTHER READING

William James. *The Varieties of Religious Experience*. New York: Longmans, Green and Co., 1902.

Herbert S. Jennings. *The Universe and Life*. New Haven: Yale University Press, 1933.

Pierre Lecomte du Noüy. *The Road to Reason*. New York: Longmans, Green and Co., 1949.

Herbert J. Muller. *Science and Criticism*. New Haven: Yale University Press, 1943.

Dr. Edmund W. Sinnott is Sterling professor of botany, chairman of the department of botany, director of the Sheffield Scientific School and chairman of the Division of Science at Yale University. He is a former president of the American Association for the Advancement of Science, the Botanical Society of America, and the American Society of Naturalists. The author of various books and pamphlets on botany and genetics, Dr. Sinnott has just completed a book to be published in the spring by the University of North Carolina Press.

3

Man and the Earth that Supports Him

KIRTLEY F. MATHER

ALTHOUGH the impact of science upon the life of man has been truly revolutionary, it has not relieved him from dependence upon the earth and its material resources. Indeed, that dependence has even been increased in modern times. The efficiency and comfort of a technologically mature culture, such as we enjoy today in American cities, requires a ceaseless flow of metals and mineral fuels from mine and quarry, pit and well, through processing plants and factories to ultimate consumers. Exhaust those mineral stores at their source, or cut off the supply anywhere along the line, and we would soon have to return to the horse-and-buggy ways of a half century ago.

The world as a whole has consumed more of its mineral stores since 1900 than in all the previous history of mankind. Since the beginning of the industrial revolution, back in the 18th century, each new advance in technology has created new needs for minerals and agricultural products. This will doubtless continue to be the pattern for man's relation to the earth throughout many future years.

Petroleum production in the United States did not amount to 100 million barrels per year until after that date. In the early 1920s it exceeded a half billion barrels per year, and fifteen years later, it reached a billion barrels per year. In 1943 the rising curve of annual production crossed the one and a half billion barrel mark and in 1948 it reached two billion barrels. Iron ore was being mined in the United States at annual rates of only about 60 million tons in the early 1920s, whereas more than 100 million tons have been mined each year since 1942.

Similarly, the per capita consumption of mechanical energy is rapidly increasing. Most of the high-speed, labor-saving machinery of our technologic age is power driven. The United States consumes about three times as much energy per person at this time as it did fifty years ago. A little more than 52 per cent of this energy is derived from coal, 44 per cent from petroleum and less than 4 per cent from water power.

RENEWABLE AND NON-RENEWABLE RESOURCES

Mineral fuels and metalliferous ores are non-renewable resources. They constitute nature's stored capital. As such natural resources are used, the stores are depleted, and eventually they will be exhausted. Water power and the agricultural resources derived from plants and animals are renewable. They constitute man's annual income. If wisely used, there need be no fear of future exhaustion. At present, mankind is relying heavily upon the non-renewable resources, but there is a definite trend toward substitution of renewable resources for the non-renewable and a shift toward relatively greater reliance upon annual income than upon stored capital. This bids fair for the future, but the change will be slow. The question is pressing, whether or not the mineral resources are adequate to meet human needs during the next half century.

No nation possesses adequate supplies of all the varied mineral resources to meet its present needs. Domestic shortages of certain substances now available in adequate quantities are very likely to develop in the next few years. The United States is dependent upon Malaya, the East Indies and Bolivia for tin, upon Canada for nickel and uranium, upon the Soviet Union for ferromanganese. Its petroleum resources have been depleted more rapidly than those of other countries, so that within a decade domestic production of crude oil will not be sufficient to meet the demands.

Thanks to science and technology, however, substitutes for some of the non-renewable resources are already available. Petroleum products, for example, may now be synthesized from coal and oil shale. The known reserves of these carbon-rich rocks in the United States are sufficient to supply the present annual demand for petroleum products for at least 2,000 years. The processes, however, are expensive and it would be desirable to import petroleum from abroad, as indeed we began to do in 1948.

RESERVES OF ESSENTIAL MINERAL RESOURCES

Taking the world as a whole, the known and probable reserves of all the essential mineral resources appear adequate to meet the world's needs for several centuries. Although certain of the richest and most accessible metalliferous ore bodies may be exhausted within a few years, there are many lower-grade deposits that may be used when and if it is necessary to rely upon them. Processes of "beneficiation," improved techniques of mechanized mining, and more effective methods of extraction or refining may make it almost or quite as economical to handle such ores in the near future as it is to extract the metals from the richer ores that are now being exploited. At the same time the potentialities of scientific research should not be underrated. In our lifetime, men have learned how to extract magnesium from sea water, where it is present in practically limitless quantities; and it is now available as a substitute for aluminum for many purposes. Intensive search for copper, lead and zinc ore bodies has not yet covered all possibilities in the United States and has scarcely begun in many geologically favorable places in several foreign lands.

There seems to be abundant basis for the expectation that scientific research and technologic development will enable future generations to secure all the required mineral fuels and metalliferous ores for the expanding needs of increasing industrialization and expanding populations during at least the next century. Beyond that it is idle to speculate. No man of science can forecast today the achievements resulting from research a hundred years hence.

The optimistic outlook for the near future is, however, based upon a world view. Valuable mineral deposits are unevenly distributed throughout the earth. Certain metals are found in only a few localities. None of the great industrial nations of the world, for example, possesses within its borders adequate supplies of tin. Mineral interdependence will doubtless change from time to time, but it will continue to be a factor with which every nation must reckon. The geology of the earth establishes the directive for free exchange of raw materials, finished products and technologic knowledge the world around, without hindrance at national boundaries.

ADEQUATE FOOD FOR THE WORLD'S PEOPLES

The world in which we live is, however, not only a world of potential abundance, with inescapable interdependence among its human inhabitants; it is also a somewhat crowded world. Its population has approximately doubled in the last hundred years, increasing from about 1.1 billion in the late eighteen forties to about 2.2 billion at the present time. Such a surge of the flood-tide of humanity has never occurred before, and it is altogether unlikely that anything like it will ever recur in the future. Nevertheless the problem of providing adequate sustenance for the rapidly growing family of human beings is a most difficult problem to solve.

Now that scientific research has made possible the fixation of atmospheric nitrogen in compounds suitable to serve as food for plants, the soil resources of the earth are at least potentially in the category of renewable resources. We may consider the soil as a factory, rather than as a storehouse. But the factory has limited capacity. Somewhat less than 20 per cent of the land surface of the globe is suitable for cultivation of crops or grazing of animals.

Much has been said in recent years about the destruction of irreplaceable soil by erosion resulting from agricultural activities. Although it is well to warn people of the very real dangers and stimulate them to adopt better ways of operating the soil factory, it would be a mistake to give the impression that a decrease in the area of arable land is inevitable. Techniques of soil conservation are now available so that the ignorance and sloth of man, not the processes of nature, must henceforth be blamed for any significant reduction in the area of crop lands available for cultivation in future years. Although the activities of men have often interfered with the processes of nature in such a way as to hasten destruction of valuable farm lands, the mistakes of the past are well understood by the soil conservation experts of today. Countless farmers have learned the virtues of contour plowing and value of cover crops. Land use is being adjusted to local conditions of soil and slope and rainfall. Already much progress has been made in many regions toward preserving the arable lands from further destruction.

Moreover, rich top-soil is not irreplaceable. Gullies may be filled with fertile silt above obstructions that check the run-off, and many abandoned farms may be returned to valuable use in a few years. Now that we know how geologic forces operate in the erosion-deposition cycle, we may take advantage of the vast healing powers of nature and restore much of the damage resulting from the ignorance and short-sightedness of the past.

INCREASING FOOD PRODUCTION PER ACRE

There yet remain many idle acres of swamp and marsh that may be drained, of arid lands awaiting irrigation, and of tropical "rain forest" that can be put to much more valuable use than at present. The extent to which the area of

arable land may be increased by such measures is essentially
a matter of economics rather than of geography. It is the
expense of building dams, constructing irrigation canals,
pumping water or digging drainage channels that sets a limit
to the dimensions of the soil factory, rather than the size
of the continents.

Balancing the many factors, it is, however, to increased
production per acre rather than to increased number of
productive acres that we now look for the greatest expansion
of the means of subsistence. Improved techniques in agrono-
my, the use of more efficient fertilizers, new types of seed,
better breeds of cattle, and eradication or control of many
diseases affecting plants or animals have worked a veritable
revolution in the agricultural output of many regions. New
varieties of wheat yield better than a hundred bushels per
acre, with no more labor, equipment or fertilizer than were
used to produce only fifty or sixty bushels per acre from the
best seed available a quarter century ago. The milk production of Europe could be increased at least 5,000,000 tons
per year, with no increase in the number of cows or of the
food for them, if mastitis were controlled by the use of
penicillin in accordance with methods of treatment, the success of which has recently been demonstrated.

THE EFFICIENT USE OF THE LAND

For many years, the United States has been a vast laboratory for scientific research not only in the more efficient use
of the land, but also in the best procedures for inspiring and
training farmers to adopt the improved methods. The results
are most encouraging. For example, the demonstration program of the Tennessee Valley Authority, begun in 1935 with
the cooperation of the United States Department of Agriculture, involved nearly 42,000 farms with a total area of more
than 6,000,000 acres. By 1942, the production of meat, eggs
and dairy products from all that acreage had increased on
the average more than 30 per cent, largely as a result of in-

creased use of mineral fertilizers rich in phosphoric
pentoxide.

The fact is that we are just beginning to apply the intelligence of science to the most fundamental task of increasing
the output of our food factory on a world-wide scale. To
take advantage of the great potentialities of the soil requires,
however, the widespread distribution of materials as well as
information. Every American, for example, should be proud
of the fact that one small item in the program of our assistance to European recovery involved the shipment of
hybrid corn to Italy. The planting of that corn in the Po
Valley during 1947 and 1948 has increased the per-acre yield
there as much as 50 per cent.

At the present time, only a small fraction of the world's
farmers is putting into practice the knowledge of agricultural procedures now available in the more enlightened
regions. If that knowledge could be spread throughout all
the farm lands of the earth and if the better strains of plants
and animals could be made available everywhere, the soil
now under cultivation could provide a high standard of
living for at least three billion people.

PROJECTION OF POPULATION GROWTH

Before we can appraise the possibilities for continuing
human progress, we must ascertain the probable demands
that future populations will place upon the limitations of
the means of subsistence as thus determined. It would be
erroneous to project the recent extraordinary growth of the
world's population into the future and anticipate that the
number of people will be doubled in the next hundred
years as it was in the last hundred years. Medical research,
since the turn of the century, has greatly lengthened the
average span of life. A large fraction of the people now
living would long since have been dead, were it not for
modern sanitation, public health measures, and medical or
surgical treatment that was entirely unavailable a century

ago. Death rates have declined while the average age of the inhabitants of all technologically progressive communities has been advancing. But this trend is now approaching its limit. In spite of all that modern medical science can do, the death rate will increase in the next few decades among such communities. We are now about "to take up the slack" resulting from the recent lengthening of the average span of life.

With the application of the intelligence of modern science to the problems of everyday life, there has invariably been a sharp increase in the rate of population growth, followed by a leveling off toward a stable condition. Certain regions have already attained what seems to be an all-time maximum of inhabitants. Others, the United States being one of them, are rapidly approaching that condition of stability in numbers. And these are the regions that enjoy the highest standard of living of all communities.

Projecting the curves of population growth from the first half of the twentieth century and applying the pattern of the white man to the future of the colored man, it would appear that the world population will become practically stable by the middle of the twenty-first century. The future maximum population of the entire world would then be in the neighborhood of three billion, certainly not more than three and a half billion.

POTENTIAL ABUNDANCE IN AN INTERDEPENDENT WORLD

There seems to be no reason for fear that, with a continuation of the present trends in the agricultural sciences, the soil resources will prove inadequate to provide a good standard of living for that prospective maximum population of the earth. Forty per cent of the inhabitants of the earth are now living under conditions to which the Malthusian principle does not seem to apply. The rate of population increase is not for them determined by any limitation upon the means of subsistence. The other 60 per cent are apparently under the Malthusian restrictions. They include the closely crowded masses of India, China and southeastern Asia. But because of ignorance and exploitation, these people are not taking full advantage of the opportunities that modern science and technology can provide for increasing vastly the means of subsistence. May it not be true that, if they are given the assistance and the freedom that they need, they too will achieve a relationship between themselves and their environment similar to that of the more fortunate 40 per cent?

The renewable resources of the soil cannot be used to best advantage without drawing heavily upon the non-renewable resources of mineral fuels and metalliferous ores—at least not in the foreseeable future of the next fifty years. Mineral interdependence will shift in degree and kind with the progress of research, but it will certainly be with us for many years to come. In an age of science and technology, no man, no community, no nation can live to itself alone. Potential abundance can be made a reality only if we accept the accompanying fact that ours is an interdependent world. The "road to survival" cannot be traversed by a small fraction of the human family if the rest are left behind.

The task we face at this midpoint of the twentieth century is difficult beyond words. To take advantage of the rich resources of our bountiful earth in such a way as to enable each inhabitant of the world neighborhood to have a fair chance for a decent standard of living will require the mobilization of all the intelligence that mankind possesses. But even that will not be enough unless there is also a great increase in the dynamic of good will. Sympathetic consideration for the rights and needs of others seems now to be an absolutely inescapable prerequisite for the successful adjustment of humanity to its environment. Mother Earth is rich enough to nourish every man in freedom, but it is by no means certain that every man is prepared to accept the responsibilities of living in freedom.

SUGGESTIONS FOR FURTHER READING

John D. Black. *Food Enough.* Lancaster, Pennsylvania: Jacques Cattell Press, 1943.

William O. Hotchkiss. *Minerals of Might.* Lancaster, Pennsylvania: Jacques Cattell Press, 1945.

Charles E. Kellogg. *The Soils That Support Us.* New York: The Macmillan Company, 1941.

Kirtley F. Mather. *Crusade for Life.* Chapel Hill: University of North Carolina Press, 1949.

Kirtley F. Mather. *Enough and to Spare.* New York: Harper and Brothers, 1944.

Fairfield Osborn. *Our Plundered Planet.* Boston: Little, Brown and Company, 1948.

William Vogt. *Road to Survival.* New York: William Sloane Associates, 1948.

Dr. Kirtley F. Mather has been professor of geology at Harvard University since 1927. From 1912-46, he was a geologist in the United States Geological Survey, and in 1919-21 he conducted explorations in Eastern Bolivia for Richmond Levering and Company. A member of many scientific organizations, among which are the Royal Geographical Society and the Geological Society of America, he is author of such books as Old Mother Earth, Science in Search of God, Sons of the Earth, Adult Education—A Dynamic Democracy *(with Dorothy Hewitt),* Source Book in Geology, *and many government bulletins, papers, and articles.*

4

The Social Sciences and the Whole Man

ORDWAY TEAD

It could be said that the social sciences are purely descriptive and objective, having nothing to do with values and goals. On the other hand, no profound scrutiny of the relation of man either to himself, to society or to the world of nature can be true if it does not take into account human aspiration and insight. Therefore, a student of the nature of man will naturally ask:

What contribution can the social sciences make in regard to man's knowledge?
How do the social sciences contribute to an understanding of the place, power and purpose of man in the world today?

The answers to these queries depend upon the purpose of the social sciences. That purpose, according to George Sarton,[1] is "to reconcile the love of truth with the love of man, the scientific spirit with the Golden Rule." We find that, by using the "love of truth" and the "love of man" as a basis for an analysis of the "whole man," a synthesis of the social sciences is obtained that discloses their value and their limitations.

THE GROWTH OF A SCIENCE OF MAN

In the first place, it is learned that the love of truth has

---

[1] *The Life of Science*, p. 145, New York, Henry Schuman, Inc., 1948.

23

already developed a science of man. Stuart Chase's *The Proper Study of Mankind* is a popular account of such knowledge. Man himself, we discover, is finally being considered as something more than either a sinner or a saint. He is being examined impersonally as a vitally important keynote of life by anthropology, economics, biology, ethics, sociology, psychology and other social sciences.

Considering the technical resources at our command, however, not much more than a commendable start has been made. In the world of medicine, for instance, as in industrial relations, agriculture, education, personal adjustments and family relations—to name the most obvious—our best scientifically known correctives are by no means being universally applied. Probably the gravest gap in the social scientist's knowledge of mankind is his present inability to overcome the lag in application of what is already known. Although the scientific method has done much during the last three centuries to raise the standard of scholarly approach to nature and man, the new knowledge has not always been sufficiently accepted or wisely applied in general use.

Within formal education there is being cultivated a scientific and rational habit of mind which will, eventually, help all people to approach all their problems in a more effective manner. Yet, it is becoming increasingly clear that the objectivity and impartiality being striven for in the natural sciences are impossible of attainment in the social sciences. A purely scientific approach to man is of little value in the latter fields of research unless there is taken into account what man himself values. It has become clearly imperative that a new kind of principle or hypothesis must enter the study of the social sciences.

HUMAN VALUES AND THE SOCIAL SCIENCES

The methods now used by the natural sciences are inadequate when applied to the dynamic details of man's struggle with social factors. Under the guise of scientific findings, there have been widely divergent contributions made by Comte, Rousseau, Darwin, Marx, Lenin, Freud and others. Their partial insight into the nature of man, although of value, has certainly not exhausted the subject as to what manner of creature man is. It has become obvious that the social scientist, simply because he loves truth, will not always move toward right answers. It is time that a more comprehensive and profound synthesis should be emerging.

The social sciences, it is apparent, will have to take into account the short-run and the long-run desires and satisfactions of man, his driving power, his aspirations. A new kind of principle must enter the study of the social sciences. The "love of man," previously mentioned, is an element in the make-up of the individual which must be considered when working toward the hypothesis now needed by the sciences of mankind. Evidently, insight into the true nature of man, instead of resulting from strictly rational analyses, will be found to be dependent upon loving sentiment and a kind of cosmic devotion.

None of the negative, destructive or demoniacal aspects of man's nature can repress the innate love of man by man. Thus it is that man is a modifier and source of his own culture while, at the same time, he is a product and expression of the culture in which he finds himself. Civilization has imposed many restraints upon man's uncontrolled emotions, actions and thoughts; but throughout history man has, nevertheless, been happiest when voluntarily assuming that role which allows him a free expression of fellow-feeling and cooperative living. It is the expanding and putting into practice of this attitude of brotherliness that permits man to merge into his generically and previously-made culture as, simultaneously, he inevitably assists in bringing into being a new and more fruitful culture.

Social heredity—the society or community upon which man is dependent—tends to produce and shape each man. But at the same time, man is able to exercise his creativeness by attempting to bring about more opportunities for the attainment of a peaceful, productive human association.

DEMOCRACY AND THE WHOLE MAN

As man finds amiability and justice in collective responsibility, he begins to enjoy the vitalizing and enriching expedients of democracy which, he discovers, is nothing more than a consequence of man's major longing to be at one with universal law. At present, democracy means for him a protective measure by which each man is viewed as an end in himself; democracy thus represents to him a basis for satisfactory and necessarily common actions. Such actions, he believes, although starting with protective statutes, eventually give scope to creative efforts which help each individual to realize beauty, morality and spirituality. In this manner, man's life, instead of being based only upon materialistic standards, awakens to a life rich and significant, a life full of practical, emancipating possibilities.

Democracy, however, as viewed historically, is the coming together of individuals in that organized manner best calculated to bring the fruits of voluntary self-subordination, opportunity for self-assumed responsibility, and for self-released creative efforts in both work and play to the greatest number of people.

Democracy, therefore, can be a channel for the active utilization of every type of science, whether natural or social. And as this cooperative method of living is applied to both man and his environment, both man and his culture must express three things—

a democrative method of living, feeling and thinking;
a scientific method of living, feeling and thinking;
and a fraternal attitude toward all persons.

It is thus that the "whole man" has a chance of being more than a promise. It is thus that he attains a harmony with the law of life itself.

The generality of men, however, still have to contend with the recalcitrance of life, its perversity, wilfulness, self-centeredness of individuals, and the fatiguing strain of "thinking for one's self." Nevertheless, nothing can permanently restrain man's value-affirming, value-seeking and value-realizing propensities.

The answers to such needs of man have been perennial and positive. This has been proved by the great procession through the centuries of prophets, seers, saviors, poets and artists who have taken mankind up to the mount of transfiguration and new vision. Man has thus found those opportunities that have enabled him to become a co-worker and co-creator with the cosmos.

And those who have become aware of the ever-present Power underlying both man and his culture know that the motivating force, behind both the "love of truth" and the "love of man," is able to unite man as a social being with a universal (scientifically authorized) Golden Rule.

SUGGESTIONS FOR FURTHER READING

Ruth Cranston. *World Faith*. New York: Harper and Brothers, 1949.

F. S. C. Northrop, Ed. *Ideological Differences and World Order*. New Haven: Yale University Press, 1949.

George Sarton. *The Life of Science; Essays in the History of Civilization*. (Life of Man Library). New York: Henry Schuman, 1948.

L. L. Whyte. *Everyman Looks Forward*. London: The Cresset Press, 1946. New York: Henry Holt and Company, 1948.

Dr. Ordway Tead has been lecturer in personnel administration at Columbia University since 1920. He is chairman of the Board of Higher Education in New York City, and also a director of Harper and Brothers. He has had wide experience as author, editor, and teacher. Some of his writings are: The Art of Leadership, New Adventures in Democracy, *and* Democratic Administration.

5

Psychology and Psychotherapy

BRAND BLANSHARD

THERE HAVE been three theories about the nature of man that have managed to remain alive for two thousand years. The first is that of Christian tradition. It says that man is a separable compound of a material, perishable body and an immaterial, imperishable soul. The second is that of a thorough-going materialism, which would reduce all the processes of mind to responses of the body. The third, an inheritance from the Greeks, holds that mind is purposive effort, struggling to rise out of a surrounding material sea and live a life of its own. In this view, mind is a matter of degree. Beginning with the lowest and simplest cell, it develops through reptile and bird and fish and quadruped and man toward a future still hidden in the clouds.

The first of these theories is on the wane. Science does not find convincing the view that a soul is affixed to the body at some pre-natal stage and can doff this body entirely when the time arrives. The real issue at the present day is between the second theory, in one of its various forms, and the third, between the materialist view on the one hand and what we may call the purposive view on the other.

THE MATERIALIST VIEW CRITICIZED

The materialist view sounds at first overwhelmingly strong. We seem to be completely at the mercy of matter.

Did we not all emerge from it a few years ago? Is it not inevitable that we shall return to it a few years hence? If our glands were to produce a tenth of a grain of thyroxin less per day, we should be promptly reduced from intelligence to moronia. A few whiffs of carbon monoxide, a stoppage for a few minutes of the flow of blood through the capillaries of our brain, and our life's expedition is abruptly halted. What exactly this matter is which holds us in its grip we do not know. The new physics has shown that it is, at any rate, a vastly more complicated stuff than we used to suppose, that every cell of our brain is a mass of millions of wavicles moving at immense velocities in complicated patterns. And the materialist argues that if only we knew enough about these mysterious wheels within wheels, we should see that in man's so-called spiritual life there is really nothing beyond them. Is the case convincing?

I do not think so. I think we can see very clearly that neither in its nature nor in its laws is mind reducible to the changes of matter.

Consider the stuff of consciousness, for example, your sensation of toothache or the color red. To say that this sensation *is* simply a current in a dental nerve, or *is* a movement of light waves of a length of 700 millionths of a millimeter, is to confuse the physical cause of a sensation with the sensation itself. The materialist version of psychology known today as behaviorism is an outgrowth of this confusion.

Materialism is also mistaken in holding that the laws which govern motion are the same as those that govern mind. In a purely material change such as the rolling of a boulder down hill, there is no trace of purposive effort or control by design. But in the debater who makes a speech, in the poet who writes a sonnet, in the thinker who solves a problem, the course of thought is quite inexplicable apart from design. The purpose or dominant end appoints the ideas that shall come up; it invites into consciousness what is relevant and excludes the irrelevant; if the thinker is master of his subject, his thought moves like an arrow to its goal. This sort of process is different absolutely from that of the rolling boulder. To deny this is to force facts into the mold of a preconceived theory.

THE PURPOSIVE VIEW OF LIFE

But if materialism will not do, where shall we turn instead? I believe that it must be to the third of our theories, to the tradition which comes down to us from the Greeks. According to Aristotle, man is a creature of three levels—if we may put it crudely, a sort of glorified layer cake. On the lowest of these levels he is a vegetable, as much as any cabbage; for his life consists in drawing nourishment from food and drink, and reproducing his kind. On the second level he is an animal; for he shares with the animal his main sensations and instincts. Above these two levels is a third, which supplies the distinctive thing about him. This, of course, is his reason, which enables him to look before and after and to act in the light of ends.

. This doctrine of levels is as true now as when Aristotle worked it out, and with the acceptance of evolution, it was seen to be enormously significant. For now it became apparent that man carried in these three levels an epitome of the history of his race. Aristotle did not know it, but man *was* once, in effect, a vegetable, then later an animal; and only aeons later still did he become a man. Just as the human embryo, in its nine months of life, climbs up the ladder of resemblance to the successive animal embryos, so the race through some thousands of centuries climbed up its own genealogical tree. Man carries in his present body the marks of his ancestry. The vermiform appendix, the third eyelid, the little hard lump near the top of our ears which marks the recession of a former tip, the slowly disappearing muscle that enables some people to move their ears, indeed many dozens of vanishing organs are the deposits of what we were a million years ago.

This holds of our minds as well as our bodies. The larger part of what we are belongs to our animal inheritance. And it seems to be roughly true that the strength of a tendency in us is proportional to the length of its animal lineage. Our reason, our sense of humor, our sense of justice, have a short history and are still imperfectly developed. On the other hand, the tendencies to fear and anger are powerful in nearly everyone and are always ready, if provoked, to burst into flame. No animal can understand the mind of man. But man can, to a great extent, understand the mind of the animal. Having known instinctive fear, we can divine by intuitive sympathy something of what the chicken feels as it seeks cover from the circling hawk, perhaps even a little about the fly that buzzes in the web as the spider moves out from its corner.

FOUR PRIMARY FREUDIAN IDEAS

It is not only racial memories that we carry in the cellars of our mind; it is also the memories of our individual past. Freud tells us that we never wholly forget any experience we have had; the effect is there and at work whether we can consciously recover it or not. We are like Christian in *Pilgrim's Progress,* carrying on our backs the growing load of our own past. This deposit from the past forms more of our self than we realize, just as there is more of an iceberg beneath the surface than we ever see above it. It is the great service of recent psychology to have explored the large dim rooms of the subconscious and shown how the ropes and wires that lead up from it affect the goings-on above. Mc-Dougall remarks that Freud has contributed more to psychology than anyone else since Aristotle; and Freud's work, as I conceive it, is to provide Aristotle with new detail. The notion of a sub-rational self with reason resting precariously on top has been taken up by Freud and worked out in masterly fashion. Let us take four of his main ideas and see how they fit into the older picture of the nature of man.

A Complex

First, the idea of a complex. A complex is merely a set of emotionally toned ideas; there is nothing necessarily abnormal about it. A man may have come to associate strong feeling with all sorts of things—his stamp collection, the Dodgers, the game of chess, above all, the person he is in love with; the ideas of these things are complexes. It is only too likely that he will then be unable to think of their objects with genuine detachment or justice. The emotions they have picked up will cling to them like clustering barnacles and, unless he takes care, will unbalance and upset his judgment. This is one of the ways in which wires from the subterranean self may make a puppet of man.

Conflict

Take, next, the notion of conflict. Inner conflict is one of the prime causes of human unhappiness. If we are bundles of impulses with varying ends, it is all but certain that some will get in the way of others; and a house divided against itself cannot stand. Harmony within is the condition of zest in work or play. A girl falls in love with a boy, but social rules decree that she must not make the fact apparent by what she does; so a conflict begins. A soldier wants to give a good account of himself in action; but he wants as much as the rest of us to stay alive, and a conflict begins which may breed mental and even physical paralysis. A man wants to be an operatic tenor, but has to sell shoes instead. If he sells the shoes with his heart on the stage, he will be like the dog in the fable who dropped the real bone for the one in the water and ended up with neither. One cannot do a job well with a mind that is wistfully gathering wool, or is restrained at every step by the brakes of reservation and doubt. "Whatsoever thy hand findeth to do, do it with thy might."

Dissociation

Thirdly, there is the idea of dissociation. When we suf-

fer from an inner conflict, one way of dealing with it is to
seal up the rival interests in tight compartments. We are all
victims of mild dissociation. As a good Christian, a man may
abhor stealing, yet feel a quiet triumph if he can do the New
Haven railroad out of a fare when the conductor fails to
notice him. On Sunday he will recite with entire belief, "I
believe in the resurrection of the body," and next day, if he
is a biologist, he will assume without question that no body,
once really dead, can be re-animated. Dissociations of this
mild kind are harmless enough. But when the incompatible
sets of complexes are at war with each other, the personality
may be split in two, and each live a life of its own. Many
of the cases in our mental hospitals belong to this type.

One classic case is that of Irene, described by Paul Janet.[1]
Irene was a poor French girl who had to watch her mother
slowly die of a malignant disease. Unable to bear the thought
of it later, she solved her problem by dissociation. Part of the
time she was her ordinary sunny self, with no memory of
what she had been through. The rest of the time she spent in
re-living the tragic days, unaware that she had now escaped
from them; the two selves took turns in controlling her
conscious mind. Dr. Prince's Sally Beauchamp,[2] in whom
there were four competing "selves," is more famous still.

Such cases make clear to us that health of mind calls for
inner unity. To judge of anything quite sanely, we must be
able to see it, not in the light of impulse, but in that of experience as a whole.

Repression

Fourth, repression. Here is another way of dealing with
conflict; we may put one side firmly out of sight. Sometimes
this succeeds; if our desire for a new car is clearly unreason-

---

[1] See *The Psychology of Insanity*, Bernard Hart, New York, The Macmillan Company, 1931.

[2] See *The Dissociation of a Personality*, Morton Prince, Longmans, Green
& Company, 1905.

able, we can repress it without damage. But sometimes the matter is harder. The soldier represses his battle experiences, but they may haunt him as uncontrollable fears. The unmarried man or woman represses sex, only to find it taking revenge in warped preoccupations with the very subject repressed, or in a too righteous indignation against those who deal with it openly. One's temper may be affected deeply by the irrational fears, attractions and antipathies that escape from one's complexes, even when these seem to be bottled up securely in the cellars of one's mind.

CONTROL OF MAN'S SUB-RATIONAL NATURE

These are a few of the ways in which our sub-rational nature may make itself felt in our conscious nature. Aristotle and Freud appear to agree as to what to do about them. Control must come through self-understanding. To bring to clear light the objects of our fears and hatreds, to look them full in the face and see them for what they are, is to deliver ourselves from their power. The man who has an unreasonable prejudice but who knows it for what precisely it is—is he really prejudiced at all?

According to this view of human nature, it is only as man recognizes his hidden desires, sees their relation to his larger goals, dismisses some wholeheartedly because he sees their unimportance, and accepts wholeheartedly the rest, that he can live a happy, zestful, and properly human life.

On this theory man *is* essentially a set of impulses ordered by reason.

SUGGESTIONS FOR FURTHER READING

Bernard Hart. *The Psychology of Insanity.* New York: The Macmillan Company, 1931.

Leonard T. Hobhouse. *The Rational Good.* London: G. Allen and Unwin, Ltd., 1921.

Josephine A. Jackson and Helen M. Salisbury. *Outwitting Our Nerves.* New York: The Century Company, 1921.

Harry A. Overstreet. *About Ourselves*. New York: W. W. Norton and Company, 1927.

Robert Henry Thouless. *The Control of the Mind*. London: Hodder and Stoughton, 1927.

Dr. Brand Blanshard is professor of philosophy and chairman of the department at Yale University. He was a Rhodes scholar, 1913-15, and Guggenheim fellow, 1929-30. He has taught at the University of Michigan, Swarthmore College and was visiting professor in philosophy at Columbia University. He is a past president of the American Philosophical Association. His writings include The Nature of Thought, Philosophy in American Education *(co-author),* Preface to Philosophy, *and numerous articles in magazines and journals.*

6

Art and the Nature of Man

MARY CECIL ALLEN

IT IS ONE of the distinguishing features of a human being
that he produces art. Animals do not paint or make sculpture; neither do they play instruments, except in a circus, or
even seem to wish to do so. Their contacts with the natural
world are physical and immediate. Man alone, it seems, is
capable of creating and receiving power and stimulus from
symbols and symbolic behavior.

Those marvels of intricacy, the nests of birds and the archi-
tectural dams of beavers, to take but two examples, are made
to type, repeated year after year, and have a definitely utili-
tarian purpose in view. Whereas, from a great antiquity or
while still in a savage stage, man has called upon his gods
and made spells by means of dances, songs, painted symbols
and images. He has considered that the potency in such actions and forms is sufficient to endow him with strength and
success or, in some cases, to deprive him of his very life. The
Second Commandment was a recognition of the image as
enchantment.

HUMAN RESPONSE TO ARTISTIC EXPRESSION

Among all man's magical arts, painting is the one which
has been accomplished with the least physical effort and the
one which also has had the most immediate effect. In common with its allied arts, there has been this strange thing

37

about painting: while the meanings attached to it have often been precise, and the reasons for its making complex and, at a later date, even incomprehensible, it has continued to work its spell on a sensitive observer without requiring previous knowledge relative to its cause or making.

The magic of painting is somehow independent of its iconography or the need that brought it into manifestation. It is not necessary to be an American Indian or a primitive African in order to receive a profound stimulus from Indian or African art. The tremendous impact of primitive African sculpture when shown in Paris early in this century and the almost immediate incorporation of its liberating message into French art are now matters of art history. The defiance of anatomy shown in those African idols may indeed have had a whole religious code behind it, but its art message— that the human mind was capable of remaking the visible world and its objects according to its own desire—was not only revealed to but understood by a group of sensitive and responsive artists. A similar instance was the great exhibition of American Indian art at the Museum of Modern Art in New York some years ago, which did not require any knowledge of archeology or any commentary to enforce its authentic power.

Without doubt, it has been one of the great mistakes of so-called "art education" to interpose a whole body of factual knowledge between the layman and the painting, the true purpose of which remains magical. Treasures of art, collected for centuries, are often considered merely as source material for historical information while their life-communicating power is overlooked. It is such groups of art that are ready to provide real and continual nourishment for the minds and hearts of all mankind without distinction of education, class or religious belief, according to each person's awareness. These collections speak a silent but universal language and provide a living link between the consciousness of the artist and that of the spectator.

WHAT DOES GREAT PAINTING TRANSMIT?

In visiting an art museum and walking through the galleries devoted in particular to paintings, one cannot help but ask: What is the nature of this vital stimulus which is transmitted by painting?

In the letters and notebooks of great painters, we have a whole documented literature on the subject of the creative process and of the efforts of the artist to induce the visitation of a concrete idea—like any magic-man of old. The artist, in modern times, is more ready than for centuries past to avow publicly the spontaneous and inspired character of his work. We find passages, for example, such as: "I discover my picture on the canvas the way a fortune teller reads the future in tea leaves."[1] And again: " . . . I . . . put on canvas the sudden apparitions which force themselves upon me. I don't know in advance . . . what colors to use."[2] These quotations are from artists whose work continues the primitive tradition of inspiration. When Braque says: "I would much rather put myself in unison with nature than copy it,"[3] he is paraphrasing the words of some of the greatest Chinese and Japanese painters of the seventeenth and eighteenth centuries. Such artists, in a way, are the last survival of the primitive seer and magician. Their gift of prophecy still exists since one finds, even in the art of more recent periods, intuitions and foresights far in advance of the level of contemporary thinking. It was not for nothing that Picasso startled Paris in 1938 by exhibiting his terrifying and inexplicable paintings of birds in cages—cages that held far too many birds, so that beaks and feathers and tails stuck out through the bars. It was interesting to watch the sensitive reaction of the French public to that exhibition. The people obviously regarded

---

[1] Henry R. Hope, *Georges Braque*, p. 150, New York, Museum of Modern Art in collaboration with the Cleveland Museum of Art, 1949.

[2] From a reported statement by Picasso in Herbert Read's *Art Now*, p. 109, London, Faber and Faber, 1948.

[3] *Cahier de Georges Braque*, p. 25, New York, Curt Valentin, 1948.

Picasso's creations as a portent, though of what, no one knew. They were silent and uneasy before the paintings.

Cubism was another case in point. Through its disintegration of objects and its broken-mirror reflection of environment in which the simultaneous vision of all planes dominated a composition, Cubism destroyed the flat photographic image and presented a new world to us. At the same time, it recorded for those who could recognize it, as with a seismatic instrument, the tremor of newly organizing apprehensions.

THE FUNCTION OF PAINTING

It is indeed the function of painting to continually remake the appearance of the world for each new generation in a kind of colored shorthand which will, at first, appear to be a hieroglyph. As long as painting adopted the "realistic" appearance of the world as part of its message, the non-painting public generally assumed the meaning to be a sort of literary illustration and appreciated it as such, passing over the magical element just as it ignored the magic in nature itself. Only the simple-hearted expected the votive painting to move. Yet in another sense, that was exactly what it was created to do—to move, not itself, but the spectator.

This moving power emanating from great paintings is a liberating and constructive force which sets up a new scheme of life, a new kind of world which has little to do with the ordinary life we live. The strange excitement it causes, when understood by a responsive person, is due to the sudden realization that there are other laws than those which govern overt human behavior; that there is a world in which the mental and intuitive nature of man can live a life of its own, according to its own internal necessity. Such a person is beginning to realize that a more vital and expansive world actually existed in embryo in him as a child and that he has never been able to completely discard or entomb it. In its undeveloped expression in the world of action, it has been, from time to time, explosive or uncontrollably destructive.

Yet when consciously aware of this deeper and more dynamic part of himself, man has found that this "magical" force, emanating especially from works of art, is capable of revealing new faculties by awakening and gradually developing hitherto latent, inner resources.

Painting, like music and the dance, is a means of conveying an idea *in its own terms,* that is, in its unchanged and original state, from person to person, so that it can affect the sensitive beholder in all its wordless immediacy and continue its development like a germ within him. This idea does more than just place him *en rapport* with the world outside him. It means for him the awakening of new internal energies containing within themselves an ordered principle of growth. In this sense, art can play an extraordinarily important part in the evolution of constructive tendencies related to human energy. Beethoven once remarked of his music that the man who understood it would be free from the misery which most men drag about with them. And Kandinsky in his book *Concerning the Spiritual in Art*[4] says of the coming artist: "He will attempt to arouse more refined emotions as yet unnamed. Just as he will lead a complicated and subtle life, so his work will give to those observers capable of feeling them, emotions subtle beyond words."

ART AIMS TO AWAKEN THE TOTALITY OF MAN

For centuries man has been willing to express, publicly at least, only the most docile and conservative sides of his nature. However, great cataclysms, such as war, have shown that he possesses other more violent and emotional potentialities which, in the succeeding times of peace, are suppressed and concealed as quickly as possible. Man as a totality is an almost unknown being. We can only conjecture his possible nature.

Art is, perhaps, the only activity which even aims at

---

[4] P. 24, New York, Wittenborn, Schultz, Inc., 1947.

awakening and bringing into activity, without reserve, the totality of man. The mysterious beauty which results from this fearlessness may well give us confidence that there is also a way in which the ordinary man can safely and constructively express his complete nature in actual daily living. The process of growth toward man's full stature, when nourished and stimulated by art, could be a most rapid one; and as art expresses its most lofty and important function, it becomes a means of evolution which, effectively developed, transforms man into a sensitive, honest and original worker—as well as observer. In fact, through art man can, by his own efforts, unlock within himself doors to new vistas where he will find himself the recipient of undreamed of, practical and emancipating attributes.

ARTISTS AND THE NON-PAINTING PUBLIC

There are, naturally, among artists themselves many different types. Some are merely skillful imitators of the objective appearance of nature or are virtuosi who dazzle by sheer technique. There are, however, those who, without ignoring technique, have transcended physical nature and mechanical scaffoldings and who work from intuitive or synthesized focal viewpoints. Kandinsky[5] has compared the world of human beings to a spiritual triangle, the segments of which, in its lowest divisions, belong to materialists of the most elementary kind, while the other segments gradually narrow upwards through the academic theorists and learned pedants of all kinds towards the great scientists, artists and philosophers. There are artists in each segment. He who can see beyond the limits of his own segment, Kandinsky says, is a prophet who helps in the advancement of others.

It is interesting to notice that painters are gradually diminishing the obvious differences between themselves and the

---

[5] *Ibid.*, p. 27.

non-painting public. They no longer adopt "bohemian" dress or haircuts in order to distinguish themselves from the crowd. Instead, they are now prophetically realizing that the powers they are using unite them with the crowd rather than separate them from it. Formerly, the artist set himself apart both by his dress and behavior and was, therefore, misunderstood and condemned by the layman for irreligious and disorganized living. Although such criticism was not warranted any more than it might have been in any other field of endeavor, the artist, it is true, always delighted in showing himself as he actually was, openly defying conventions which he had good reason to despise. This came from his innate pride in asserting his bond with nature and disdain for that which was false or for those who timidly accepted artificial concepts or hollow social observances.

ART AND WORLD UNITY

During the last decade, there has been a great change in the feeling of the general public, as well as in the attitudes of the world of art. There has been an increased interest and harmony in that sphere of creativeness. One reason for this new era in art is that a tremendous number of "spectators" have voluntarily raised themselves to the artist's level. In fact, the professional pride of the academic artist has been rather badly shaken by the number of laymen who, having entered the art field, have gradually proved their ability to contact the same power which these artists had previously considered a monopoly of their own rather exclusive circle. Laymen, with comparatively little training, now know that art is a natural activity and that a rigid professional training in the imitation of objects of "physical" nature is no longer an essential for art expression or for an understanding of nature itself. Moreover, in a technical sense, it has become much less "difficult" to paint, for the conception of painting as a verifiable record of people, landscapes and objects has diminished. This has helped to elimi-

nate the barriers which bound painting to any one nationality, class or period. Painting, on the other hand, has finally
entered every phase of human life; it has learned to be perfectly human. Due to this liberalizing tendency within painting itself, the creative action of colors and forms, apart from
all directly imitative effect, is having its most direct and no-
ticeable impact upon the remaining spectators.

Nevertheless, in a way, one might have thought that the
gap between painters and the public would have been greater
than formerly since the tremendous freedom accepted by the
modern artist to distort and change appearances might have
presented to the layman insuperable difficulties. But the
exact opposite has been the result. The sensitive spectator is
now beginning to feel the full meaning of artistic expression as a human faculty. No longer distracted and over-awed
by its details and trimmings, he is beginning, however dim-
ly, to recognize the potential artist in himself and to respond
to those inner freedoms.

This is an advance, however slight and necessarily limited,
in the direction of world unity. The practice and deep appreciation of art as a form of human development in which the
whole nature of man is brought into play, can bring people
together, not by their needs, their fears and their miseries,
but by their best faculties, their growing awarenesses.

SUGGESTIONS FOR FURTHER READING

Mary Cecil Allen. *The Mirror of the Passing World*. New York: W. W.
Norton and Company, 1928.

Mary Cecil Allen. *Painters of the Modern Mind*. New York: W. W.
Norton and Company, 1929.

Guillaume Apollinaire. *The Cubist Painters* (Aesthetic Meditations,
1913). Documents of Modern Art. New York: Wittenborn, Schultz,
Inc., 1944.

Wassily Kandinsky. *Concerning the Spiritual in Art*. Documents of
Modern Art. New York: Wittenborn and Company, 1947.

José Ortega y Gasset. *The Dehumanization of Art.* Princeton: Princeton University Press, 1948.

Problems of Contemporary Art. New York: Wittenborn and Company, Inc., 1945-1949.

Wolfgang R. Paalen. *Form and Sense.* 1945.

Herbert Read. *The Grass Roots of Art.* 1949.

Alexander Dorner. *The Way Beyond Art.* The Work of Herbert Bayer. 1947.

Possibilities. Vol. I. 1947-1948.

G. Vantongerloo. *Paintings, Sculptures, Reflections,* 1948.

Otto Rank. *Art and Artist.* New York: Alfred A. Knopf, 1932.

***

Miss Mary Cecil Allen, one of Australia's leading modern artists, has been a lecturer and teacher of painting in both the United States and France. While acting as instructor of art (1931-1945) for Miss Hewitt's Classes in New York City, she exhibited her own work at Wildenstein's Gallery, the Metropolitan Museum of Art and the annual art shows in Provincetown, Massachusetts. Among her writings are The Mirror of the Passing World and Painters of the Modern Mind. At present, Miss Allen is en route to Australia where exhibits of her paintings will be held in Melbourne and Sydney.

7

Religious Disciplines (The West)

JOHN SUTHERLAND BONNELL

ONE OF THE latest developments in medical science is to regard the patient as a person, an entity of body, mind and spirit. These act and react upon each other. If a malady attacks one of these, it will make its influence felt upon the other two.

Hawthorne in *The Scarlet Letter* writes: "A bodily disease which we look upon as whole and entire within itself may, after all, be but a symptom of some ailment in the spiritual part." It is also true, as Lucretius says:

> For when the body's sick and ill at ease,
> The mind doth often share in the disease.

These considerations help to underline the importance of religious disciplines. Einstein has pointed out that science itself is founded on a great unprovable assumption: that the external world apprehended by man's senses is real.

THE MAJOR ASSUMPTION OF RELIGION

Religion, also, has its assumptions, the major one of which is that God and man are essentially alike in mental and spiritual structure. If that were not true, there could neither be science nor revelation. There could be no science, because, in that case, it would be impossible for man to understand the universe; and there could be no revelation be-

47

cause God could not manifest himself to man or establish communion with him.

The fact is that man's mind is a counterpart of the Creator's. Man finds rationality in the universe, a rationality which responds to that which resides in himself. He can formulate the laws of the universe because it is the work of mind.

If, as we believe, creation is a mirror of God, it is also a mirror in which man sees his own face. Man was created with an aptitude for God. Revelation is possible only because of this kinship between God and man, which enables the Creator to reveal himself to the creature.

This affinity between God and man has been superbly expressed in that statement[1] by fifteen eminent American scientists, including Henry Fairfield Osborn, Michael Pupin, William A. Noyes, Jr., Edwin Grant Conklin, and Robert A. Millikan: "It is a sublime conception of God which is furnished by science and one wholly consonant with the highest ideals of religion when it represents Him as revealing Himself through inbreathing of life into its constituent matter, culminating in man with his spiritual nature and all his God-like powers."

THE DISCIPLINE OF PRAYER

One of the most important of religious disciplines is prayer. Its profound and transforming influence can be demonstrated in the life of individuals.

For several years, each week I have met with a group of approximately fifteen persons who have been experimenting with prayer. It is nothing short of extraordinary to witness the steady growth in spiritual stature of these people. This experiment provides also a demonstration of the efficacy of group therapy.

Spiritual discipline has been of incalculable assistance to

---

[1] Henry F. Osborn, *The Earth Speaks to Bryan*, p. 87, New York, Charles Scribner's & Sons, 1925.

alcoholics as they seek to gain self-mastery. The first three of the Twelve Steps in Alcoholics Anonymous are illuminating:

1. We admitted we were powerless over alcohol—that our lives had become unmanageable.
2. We came to believe that a Power greater than ourselves could restore us to sanity.
3. We made a decision to turn our will and our lives over to the care of God *as we understood Him.*

Thousands of former alcoholics gladly testify that that Power helped them to turn defeat into victory.

One of the founders of Alcoholics Anonymous, in an address to the Medical Society of the State of New York, said: "If the spiritual content of the Twelve Steps is actively denied, they can seldom remain dry. That is our A.A. experience everywhere. We stress the spiritual simply because thousands of us have found that we can't do without it."

PSYCHIATRIC WORK AND SPIRITUAL DISCIPLINES

Spiritual disciplines have supplemented the work of psychiatrists by achieving a synthesis after the analysis of a patient's problem. Psychiatric experience reveals that often after an analysis, synthesis has not been achieved. There is abundant evidence of the achievement of a synthesis through spiritual disciplines when secular therapy had failed.

A well-known psychiatrist in the eastern United States says: "There is considerable question as to whether integration solely on the psychological level is really integration at all."

Frequently a passage of Scripture acts as a kind of catalyst in achieving synthesis.

"If God be for us, who can be against us?" (Romans 8:31)

"The Lord is on my side, I will not fear. What can man do unto me?" (Psalm 118:6)

"I can do all things through Christ, who strengtheneth me." (Philippians 8:13)

Spiritual discipline, by employing confession and the received forgiveness of God, has accomplished far-reaching results in the lives of many people. I am not referring here to neurotic guilt, but to what Dr. Karl Menninger describes as "moral guilt": a transgression of an explicit moral law. In many such instances, providing a psychiatric "out" or assuring the patient that he was ill at the time of his transgression, and other means of evading the issue, will likely fail. This is especially true if the individual has received a religious upbringing with a strong moral emphasis. The received forgiveness of God lifts a great burden from the human heart, and turns the penitent to a new and better life. It releases hope and confidence, and arouses the spirit of thanksgiving. It lays stress upon the better future that is opening up before the penitent, rather than upon the past.

"Forgetting the things that are behind," says St. Paul, "and reaching forth to those that are before, I press toward the mark for the prize. . . . " (Philippians 3:13-14)

FAITH AND PHYSICAL ILLNESS

In the case of a physical illness, too, spiritual disciplines may well play a determinative role. This is particularly true in the case of patients preparing for an operation. They are relieved of dread and fear, and the consequent strain on the heart is greatly reduced. A trustful, calm, prayerful state of mind reduces blood pressure, and so prepares the patient that anaesthesia is produced more readily. The distressing after-effects of an operation are often mitigated. In all such cases, convalescence is more rapid and less eventful.

There is little doubt that in cases of critical illness, where the will to live is weakened, spiritual discipline has restored hope and confidence. Even more important is the power of faith and prayer to keep people healthy and sane and in an untroubled frame of mind. It resolves the dark riddle of hidden fears and destructive inner regressions and buried resentments.

The one indispensable element of all true healing is faith, that mighty spiritual force that eludes the test tube and the methods of the laboratory, and yet provides inexhaustible reserves of energy for human welfare. As medical science abandons its materialism and the Church recovers from its fear of scientific truth, the physicians of the body and the physicians of the spirit will find a common basis for the fullest cooperation. Together, they will explore the marvelous effects produced by an active faith and utilize these in maintaining the health of those who are well and in healing those who are ill. Then the no man's land between science and religion, which has been a prolific breeding ground for all manner of extreme healing cults, will be cleared away, and medicine and religion will find a common goal in God's purposes for the well-being of His children.

SUGGESTIONS FOR FURTHER READING

John Sutherland Bonnell. *Pastoral Psychiatry.* New York: Harper and Brothers, 1938.

John Sutherland Bonnell. *Psychology for Pastor and People.* New York: Harper and Brothers, 1948.

J. A. C. Murray. *An Introduction to a Christian Psychotherapy.* New York: Charles Scribner's Sons, 1938.

John Rathbone Oliver. *Psychiatry and Mental Health.* New York: Charles Scribner's and Sons, 1932.

Karl R. Stolz. *The Church and Psychotherapy.* New York: Abingdon-Cokesbury Press, 1943.

Leslie D. Weatherhead. *Psychology and Life.* London: Hodder and Stoughton, 1934.

Dr. John Sutherland Bonnell has been pastor of The Fifth Avenue Presbyterian Church since 1935. After graduating from divinity school, he was pastor of a number of large Canadian churches, the last of which was Westminster Church in Winnipeg. In 1941 he went to Great Britain as goodwill ambassador to British churches, representing the General

Assembly of the Presbyterian Church of the United States. Dr. Bonnell has counseled thousands of people needing spiritual rehabilitation, and has written a number of books on pastoral psychology. He is lecturer on the "Cure of Souls" at Princeton University and has written many articles for religious periodicals on the subject. An active speaker on the radio for the past decade, he has for some years carried on a nationwide radio ministry on "National Vespers."

8

Religious Disciplines (The East)

TARAKNATH DAS

ALL RELIGIONS DEAL with man's relations with the Universal Spirit which, although acknowledged to be One, is designated by many different names. The nature of man, however, seems to be more difficult to define since an understanding of it leads back again to the Universal Spirit and necessitates a more detailed study of that Oneness. The result of such knowledge reveals that the most profound concepts of divinity are unanimous in considering man as something more than a material object. Man, such analyses disclose, is Spirit, and, in his essence, he is Soul. For instance, we find in reading Plato's *Phaedo* that Socrates discussed the matter in this manner with Cebes:

> "Is not the conclusion of the whole matter this," Socrates asks of Cebes, "that the soul is in the very likeness of the divine, and immortal, and intellectual, and uniform, and indissoluble and unchangeable; and the body is in the very likeness of the human, and mortal, and unintellectual, and multiform, and dissoluble and changeable. Can this be denied?"

And Cebes answers, "No, indeed."

This conception leads one to believe that man, instead of being confined to the physical machine regarded as the body, is in reality a divine and immortal soul which is using a physical body. This viewpoint, held by Socrates and Plato, had also been voiced by sages of ancient India whose wisdom, relative to this concept, is revealed in many passages in the sacred literature of the Hindus. For instance, in the *Bhagavad Gita,* the following statements are found:

> Even as a person casts off worn-out clothes and puts on others that are new, so the embodied Self casts off worn-out bodies and enters into others that are new.

> Weapons cut It (Soul) not; fire burns It not; water wets It not; the wind does not wither It.

> This Self cannot be cut nor burnt nor wetted nor withered. Eternal, all-pervading, unchanging, immovable, the Self is the same forever.

> The Self is said to be unmanifest, incomprehensible, the unchangeable. Therefore, knowing It to be so, you should not grieve.

In the *Upanishads,* we find that the aspects of the Universal Spirit *(Brahman)* are Absolute Existence *(Sat),* Absolute Consciousness *(Chit)* and Absolute Bliss *(Anandam),* and the assertion that the Self (man conceived as Soul) is, in its essence, *Brahman* or Universal Spirit. Thus we read:

> Brahman is Being, Consciousness and Infinity.

> In the beginning there was That only which is One only without a second. It is True. It is the Self. And thou art It.

MAN'S SEARCH FOR INNER PEACE AND TRUE HAPPINESS

With this understanding of his spiritual nature, man possesses the key to his survival, emancipation and true happiness or bliss. Although he may have a finely coordinated body, such an instrument is not, in itself, much more ingenious than a machine which calculates difficult mathematical problems and points toward the source of all motion, beauty and sensibility. But this does not directly take into account such qualities as love, wisdom or virtue.

One of the most interesting facts about man's nature is that, since he is not satisfied with mere material possessions or surroundings, he is, spasmodically at least, in search for inner peace and true happiness—for liberation from his own

self-imposed bonds. This search for happiness is clearly expressed in Plato's *Symposium,* where the following conver-
sation is held between Diotima, a woman wise in many
kinds of knowledge, and Socrates. She begins by asking:

"When a man loves the beautiful, what does he desire?"

Socrates answers: "That the beautiful be his."

"Still," Diotima continues, "the answer suggests a further
question which is this: What is given by the possession of
beauty?"

"That," Socrates replies, "is a question to which I have no
answer ready."

"Then let me put the word 'good' in place of the beautiful and repeat the question." And then she adds, "What
does he who loves the good desire?"

Socrates responds, "The possession of the good."

Diotima inquires, "And what does he gain who possesses
the good?"

Socrates replies, "Happiness. There is no difficulty in
answering that question."

Thus one may say that the ever-presence of spiritual nature is the cause of man's quest for true happiness. Alcibiades
once remarked: "The wise physician, skilled in healing our
wounds, shall prescribe, and we shall obey." This injunction
implies that we should obey certain spiritual laws laid down
by those who have attained God-consciousness. The statement also suggests that certain physicians mistake a satis-
faction of the sensual side of physical life for happiness.
These physicians of the soul follow a profession of materialism and, in attempting to cure inner maladies, often make
them worse because of a disregard of spiritual laws.

A HINDU METHOD TO ATTAIN INNER PEACE

The process of achieving a truly blissful state of inner
peace has been thoroughly investigated and analysed by the
sages of India. One of the methods by which such happiness

is attained is known as *Raja Yoga*. Its practice necessitates a concentrated mindfulness which might not, in the West, be associated with the term happiness. There are eight stages or approaches to this spiritually moral training which leads to inner peace. They are:

1. *Yama:*   The control of the lower nature of man. In a negative sense, not to do that which might degrade.

2. *Niyama:*   The observance of rules or moral laws. This is the positive side of *Yama*.

3. *Asana:*   The science of the correct seated posture for meditation.

4. *Pranayama:*   These are breathing exercises which cannot be explained in words, they can only be attempted or mastered while under the supervision of a *Guru,* a spiritual guide.

5. *Pratyahara:*   The elimination of certain contents from the mind.

6. *Dharana:*   The holding fast to certain thought contents in the mind.

7. *Dhyana:*   Meditation.

8. *Samadhi:*   The state of spiritual consciousness.

Here we have what might be termed the religious or spiritual disciplines which any man who is interested in the control of animal instincts might follow. The spiritual consciousness which is awakened and brought into action by such training may be the motivating power for all human activities.

Hindu philosophers are quite cognizant that there are various types of individuals. There are some who express inertia or laziness *(tamas),* others who have an active temperament *(rajas),* while there are those who obviously possess blissfulness or illumination *(sattva).* Of course, these qualities, in varying degrees, are found in each individual; but, for the most of us, in order to attain illumination, discipline and training of *sattvic* or blissful qualities are necessary.

It is imperative that man be jolted or forced out of a state of laziness since the rising above inertia is the first requisite of a spiritual life. Laziness is almost synonymous with ignorance which, in turn, leads to "egotism," among the selfish expressions of which are unreasonable attachments or aversions, together with a so-called love of a physical life. The offspring of such attitudes and desires are, from the standpoint of spiritual training, afflictions.

FREEDOM FROM AFFLICTIONS

It is unreasonable to expect true happiness in this life when one is enslaved by afflictions which have been caused by ignorance and false standards. The first step toward inner and outward bliss is for one to ask the question: How may I get rid of afflictions? In this instance, the answer is more simple than the accomplishment; but freedom may be experienced through the practice of religious and spiritual disciplines. By adherence to those physical, emotional and mental guides which have previously been listed, a person may attain a calm, yet positive, poise which will enable him to control his physical and emotional vehicles. He then becomes at peace with himself and the universe and, as a consequence, his forces and talents gradually begin to be used for the serving of others—as well as himself—and he learns to perform that duty which is his in the immediate present according to his station or stage of evolution in life. At all times, he acts with non-attachment, no longer a slave to his desires.

Thus it has been said that one must possess right desires, thoughts and ideals. *Rise above your desires; be a master of yourself*—such is the secret of real freedom, although some modern psychologists and psychoanalysts might argue that this is a doctrine of repression. There is no room for repression in self-illumination. Instead, there is the essential necessity of pursuing a course of life which will lead to self-regeneration. License, many times, is an excuse for the abuse of freedom, and an unrestrained and misdirected sensuous life cannot bring genuine freedom or an inner peace. Mere pursuit of material enjoyment cannot produce emancipation of any kind. Whereas illumination, which can throw the right light or understanding upon every phase of man's activity, is ready now to be bestowed on any man whose *"happiness is within, whose relaxation is within, whose light is within." (Bhagavad Gita)* The one who follows religious disciplines is the recipient of spiritual strength sufficient to meet every obstacle; he is given that spiritual force which enables him to overcome indolence, indecision, carelessness, mistaken notions and even disease—physical or mental.

FREEDOM WITHOUT FEAR

A free man is one who has advanced to a state of consciousness in which there is no fear. The limitations imposed by fear dissolve in ratio to the realization of the consciousness of the Universal Spirit. As is true with the removal of other restrictions, being fear-less is a result of the discipline which opens the way to an ever-present resource of spiritual Goodness and to a recognition of God-in-man.

Although this is a process of "self-surrender," it has nothing to do with inaction or fatalism. From the *Bhagavad Gita* are the following words, "O Lord, Thou residing in my innermost being, I shall follow thy bidding in whichever way thou mayest direct me." And in the Lord's Prayer we find the affirmation, "Thy will be done," which means—may I become the instrument to carry out the Divine Will. This is a surcharging of the self with the limitless strength emanating from the Divine.

WORLD PEACE AND RELIGIOUS DISCIPLINES

When the time comes that man is no longer seeking for peace but, instead, is Peace, then he will not only be at peace with the peoples on this globe and in harmony with the universe; he will be able to instruct and guide his fellow-man toward that peace which he, himself, has realized. This will be only one result of his religious disciplines. It is surely time that we all knew that man is more than a machine or only a physical body, for there is related to the nature of man this spiritual aspect of living. However, this spiritual aspect of human nature cannot be explained; it must be experienced, and each man can do that for himself if he is willing to submit to and abide by religious disciplines.

Those who are in search of world peace should remember that, although men can form organizations, organizations by themselves cannot produce men of peace. It is true that men . are able to use certain organizations for the furtherance of the cause of peace; but without the peaceful intent of the "inner man" within each one of us, there cannot be peace. Thus the cultivation of religious and spiritual disciplines is vital to the cause of world peace.

SUGGESTIONS FOR FURTHER READING

Claude Bragdon. *Yoga and You.* New York: Alfred A. Knopf, 1943.

Alexis Carrel. *Man, The Unknown.* New York: Harper and Brothers, 1935.

J. W. Hauer. *Der Yoga Als Heilweg.* Stuttgart: Verlag von W. Kohl-hammer, 1932.

Swami Nikhilananda. *The Bhagavad Gita.* New York: Ramakrishna-Vivekananda Center, 1944.

Swami Nikhilananda. *The Upanishads.* Volume I. New York: Harper and Brothers, 1949.

Swami Vivekananda. *Raja Yoga.* New York: Ramakrishna-Vivekananda Center, 1933.

Ernest Wood. *Practical Yoga.* A new translation with commentary of the Yoga Aphorisms of Patanjali. New York: E. P. Dutton, 1948.

Dr. Taraknath Das is a native of India and became a United States citizen in 1914. He is Watumull Foundation visiting professor at the

Institute of Public Affairs and Regional Studies, New York University, and lecturer, Department of History, Columbia University. Author and publicist, he has held lecturing posts in international affairs at Catholic University, College of the City of New York, University of Maryland, and Queens College, Flushing. He is author of many books and articles, some of which are: Asia's Part in War and Peace, Foreign Policies of President Franklin D. Roosevelt, Essays on World Politics, *and* Requisites for Better Understanding Between East and West. *He was selected for the Hall of Fame at the New York World's Fair, 1940.*

9

Man and His Destiny

GARDNER MURPHY

It might be possible to take some little corner of this vast problem, "man and his destiny," and to show how the various forms of research with which we are now concerned may point toward larger implications and answers which go beyond that little corner which today we have made secure.

I would not have the arrogance to define for you technically what man's destiny is or even the direction in which our research should move, but I would venture to try to bring together three kinds of evidence, of which psychical research is one, and to show how psychical research fits in with the data of the other two.

THE PRINCIPLES OF COMPETITION AND INTERDEPENDENCE

The first of the trends which I want to stress, which has its close interrelations with psychical research, is the study of biological evolution, the process which Charles Darwin defined in his *The Origin of Species* in the middle of the last century. For a long time we were given to understand that the "survival of the fittest" was simply a competitive principle—that individual living things compete for existence and, by their living, crowd out others which must die.

But during the last fifteen or twenty years, the experimental research of many biologists, such as W. C. Allee[1] of

---

[1] In *The Social Life of Animals,* Warder C. Allee, New York, W. W. Norton and Company, 1938.

the University of Chicago, has stressed the fact that interdependence or fellow-feeling among members of a biological group is just as fundamental and just as basic as individual competition; and has pointed out that cooperation and social integration is as important in the evolutionary process as competition. In these terms, we begin to take much more seriously the actual evidence of fellow-feeling, of out-reaching or positive responses. As we watch behavior in early childhood, we no longer assume that each individual will inevitably push himself ahead and crave every toy or every attention he can get; instead, we begin to ask if there is something in our society that does not satisfy the child's needs and, therefore, makes it aggressive.

This basic principle which biologists define for us is seen in many species lower than man. One might say that cohesion is a general biological tendency; individuals may work toward "mutual aid" (Kropotkin)[2] rather than toward the destruction of others. This is one of the things we must take into account when we think of "man and his destiny." Data which mean the most, in relation to this tendency, define not only the nature of the isolated individual but the relation between two or more individuals, in other words, that which makes one man reach out toward another. The field with which we are primarily concerned is the relation between persons, and we are looking more and more for the meaning of that basic understanding which binds people together.

In the early days of psychical research, the experimental study of telepathy, or the transfer of ideas or feelings from one man to another, was assumed to be the study of certain specially gifted individuals. When a carefully planned experiment at long distance showed that certain people could succeed in identifying the pictures or words being looked at by other people, this was considered a gift or psychic po-

---

2 See *Mutual Aid*, Prince Petr Kropotkin, first published at the beginning of the present century. Reissued by Penguin Books, 1939.

tentiality with which some individuals happened to be endowed, in the same sense as they might have exceptionally good discrimination of tones or colors. More and more, it has become evident that we are dealing with interrelations. Psychical research as it has turned out is largely a study of interrelations of persons.

EXAMPLES OF SPONTANEOUS TELEPATHY

First, I want to give two examples of what I mean by spontaneous telepathy. Mrs. Severn was sleeping late one morning. About nine-thirty she was awakened by a violent blow on the mouth. She reached immediately for her handkerchief to see if her lip was bleeding. She did not know what in the world could have happened, knowing there was no one in the room. She was puzzled over the matter for a long time. About an hour and a half later, her husband, who had been boating, returned, holding a handkerchief over his mouth. She asked what was wrong and, when he removed the handkerchief, it was evident that he had been badly hit. At about nine-thirty that morning, the tiller of his boat had suddenly swung over and had caught his lip.

Now such cases are pretty common. What is the meaning of this Severn case? It seems to be a form of communication between persons who care about each other. There was no way out there on the lake for Mr. Severn to send word to his wife that he had been hurt. There was no way in which he could reach out and make a contact. Or *was* there really no way? There was a way which our own civilization has ignored. But here we have, I believe, a process resembling the process described by Allee,[3] a form of interdependence binding individuals together and making them responsive to one another.

Recently, in the *Journal of the American Society for Psychical Research,* a case was published concerning a young man, Mr. Hayworth, who had been teaching an astronomy

---

[3] *Op. cit.*

class in Dallas and had come home late in the evening. In a leisurely way he sat on the edge of his bed for a moment. Then, casually turning his head, he saw his father in the room, extending his hand to him. The father wore working clothes and there were a ruler and calipers in his breast pocket. The son thought that his father, who resided in California, had arrived on a surprise visit; but as he rose to shake his father's hand, the apparition disappeared. A moment later, a Western Union messenger came up the path, rang the bell and delivered a telegram. The father had died that afternoon. When word came later by mail from the mother, her letter stated that the young man's father had been working on their car and that a ruler and calipers had been in the breast pocket of the working clothes which he had been wearing. Perhaps a few of you have had such an experience. Did you make a record of it? May we see the record? I would beg all of you, if this area of research has any implications or fascination for you, to keep in mind the need we have for fresh reports, honest and complete analyses of what goes on during such an experience.

FELLOW-FEELING AND SPONTANEOUS TELEPATHY

There was something in the Hayworth case that is lacking in the Severn case, the fact of death. This is one of the commonest features of spontaneous telepathy. As a matter of fact, death coincidences are many times as frequent as we should expect them to be in terms of the general death rate (we rule out, of course, cases where illness or danger could be inferred). Cases involving death are more common than the death rate in the population of the Western world. But what is suggested by such cases is that there is something about death which acts in a special way, that stimulates this telepathic process.

Let us keep this in mind and see if we can fit it into a larger picture. So far, we have two kinds of evidence that point in the same direction. The first was the community of members of a species. The second was spontaneous telepathy. Both types of experience seem to point to the importance of primitive fellow-feeling, leading to a craving to understand, to take hold together and to share. People may lose their sharply defined awareness of self and self-interest. For example, we all have seen in war-time, and in community projects against disease and other enemies of human welfare, the individual sharing with others the utmost of danger and hardship, thus finding fulfillment in group loyalty.

PSYCHIATRY AND PSYCHICAL RESEARCH

I might stress, in this connection, that psychiatrists are studying all of these same facts. Erich Fromm's *Escape from Freedom* shows how man's neurotic suffering springs very largely from the loneliness which has seized upon him. Whatever one's personal tragedy in the medieval period, each man had a place. With the disintegration of the manorial system, men lost their status, became lonely individualists. Men could rise or fall but could no longer find their place in the group. From this has followed a sense of isolation. My success may be your failure. Modern man is sick because he is isolated; any success of one has to be the failure of another.

Ordinarily we do not connect these psychological facts with the facts of psychical research. However, we must not forget that psychical research is as yet in its veriest infancy. If psychical powers do exist, if they are a part of human nature, then surely their study becomes of the greatest importance, for here we are on the threshold of the discovery of a new force—a force just as new as electricity or magnetism—and one that more vitally concerns us.

Yet man is not the kind of creature that can be studied solely by the method of fractionation. The Freudians seem to have shown that much pathology, from our most trivial mistakes to a cherished delusion, is due to the operation of conflicting forces. But conflict between man and man also causes mental ill health. This is basically what produces failure of integration between human beings, produces a failure at all levels even within the individual's make-up. Just so, we find in psychical research that a little fear, a little suspicion, a little barrier between two people, as between a person and the experimenter, can block the communication which has been started.

Lawrence K. Frank,[4] discussing the "cost of competition," points out the waste in our human society that proceeds from the concentration of power; the benefits of concentration, through increased efficiency, are largely washed away by the enormous wear and tear that comes from the insecurity in the struggle to hold up one's head. The craving for security is one of the deepest and most fundamental instincts of man. It follows that we shall have to try to introduce a social order not based upon competition. This does not in itself tell us whether we have to come through blood and fire to achieve human unity or whether we may find a social solidarity and a cooperative commonwealth through slow evolutionary methods. But mankind cannot permanently expect to live in isolation.

THE DEVELOPMENT OF EXPERIMENTAL SCIENCE

Now my main emphasis is not upon this political problem but upon the deeper implications which psychical research may have as to what man really is; and the conclusion as to the kind of future for which he may be destined. I think we have got to be perfectly clear on this point: the method of science which has been with us for about three hundred years. The Greeks, of course, used experimental methods some two thousand years ago but much of their work was forgotten or ignored. Experimental science as a system of thought has been with us only about three hundred

---

[4] "The Cost of Competition" in *Society As the Patient*, New Brunswick, Rutgers University Press, 1948.

years. This science emphasized at first the problem of mechanics, the problem of mass moving in time and space, as advanced by Copernicus in the sixteenth century and by Galileo and Newton in the seventeenth. Then came the study of magnetism and of light; later still came experimental psychology as a field of experimental inquiry, rather than mere speculation, and psychical research; both are now from seventy to one hundred years of age and their results are as yet just a little speck here and there. Even in orthodox psychology you cannot always obtain much support in the universities. In psychical research you encounter every type of fear and suspicion, and it needs intelligent public support even more desperately than psychology does.

HUMAN ACTIVITY WITHIN A COOPERATIVE ATMOSPHERE

I want to speak now of a kind of research which deals directly with the question whether the individual functions · better in a cooperative than in a competitive atmosphere. If the answer is *yes*, then it is basic to the thesis I am trying to develop. The first line of work is that of Kurt Lewin who, until his recent death, was working at the Massachusetts Institute of Technology, following up a pioneer study which he had begun to develop at the State University of Iowa. His experiments dealt with the democratic process. How Thomas Jefferson would have pricked up his ears at such a suggestion! Jefferson had accepted democracy as a philosophy of life; but in our age of technology, it becomes necessary to define democracy so that we can experiment upon it by the methods of science. If it is true that fellow-feeling and cooperation improve human action, then we can show positively the value of democracy.

In one of Lewin's war-time experiments, where a group of women textile workers were already working at their maximum capacity, the question was asked whether they could not do more than they were doing. Although they were working at what was called the "physiological" limit, one of Lewin's pupils was assigned to the problem. He went in and defined what he considered to be the problem in this plant and, after making his investigation, asked the women workers to get together and discuss how much they wanted to produce, and to set a *group goal*. After a half hour of such discussion, they started working to achieve that which they, themselves, had agreed should be the essential standard for future production. Immediately the women raised their work to a level far higher than before, and they maintained their new level throughout the whole experimental period of six months. Now in what sense had they been working at a "physiological" limit? They had felt they were working as well as they possibly could. But when they defined a group goal, made a group decision about a common goal, they were able to work *collectively* toward it. Over and over again it has been possible to work out, as in this case, the conditions under which a democratic process can achieve more than a competitive process.

PEOPLE INVOLVED IN THE DEMOCRATIC PROCESS

Another problem that Lewin worked on was defined by the National Research Council Committee on Food Habits. The committee hoped that housewives would begin to make use of unpopular cuts of meat which were in abundance but which most people thought were not suitable cuts to serve. In one experiment, a group of housewives received technical instruction from a nutritionist who explained the amount of proteins, fats and vitamins to be found in these unpopular cuts. But two weeks later a "public opinion" study showed that there had been no change in actual buying habits. In another experiment, a nutritionist simply made herself available as a consultant. When housewives made inquiries of her, she answered them indirectly by asking, "What do *you* want to do in regard to the meat shortage during the war?", or "What do *you* want to do in regard to contributing to the war effort?" In this way, the housewives made their own decisions. Two weeks later, many of the women had actually bought and served the unpopular cuts.

You can see in a variety of ways that allowing people to work through a democratic process rather than as isolated individuals is not merely idealistic but very practical. A number of us were working during the war period in trying to define a cooperative research project bearing on international, interracial, and interreligious issues. Today one finds the social scientist working with Unesco, with the Economic and Social Council of the United Nations and with other agencies, using such techniques as Lewin introduced, and thus attempting to make the democratic process more useful. Even with the deterioration in our relations with the Soviet Union, it has been of interest to see here and there the disappearance of hostility. Certainly not very much is being done in comparison with what is needed but the research spirit is at work. The point I want to stress, as it has been emphasized by some large foundations recently, is that good will has to be implemented by scientific method. We not only need good will but systematic and authentic social science.

THE BASIC INTERRELATIONSHIP OF THE HUMAN FAMILY

Individual personalities fulfill themselves through the contact which they make with others. You may visualize the different individuals of the human species as islands. You may recall the poet's saying, "No man is an island," and emphasize the fact that there is a basic communication between us all; the rise and fall of water around the "islands" makes it possible to discover the unity which would otherwise be unguessed. From this point of view, you may get a great deal of information from psychical research as well as psychology and may know that, in reality, "We are all members one of another" as St. Paul said. We all have a basic unity as members of a fellowship.

Hypotheses like these may be called "prophetic generalizations." Some will think that the majestic intensity of prophetic genius is lowered by studying it scientifically. Yet each hypothesis must be formulated in such a way that it leads one to make straightforward experimental tests. Every form of communication which modern science can define in terms of experimental tests needs to be studied. From such a point of view psychical research takes its place with many other investigations in trying to find the integration of the human family. This can be more effective than trying only to achieve integration within the individual personality. Individual personality is better understood when it is seen in terms of membership in the social group.

SUGGESTIONS FOR FURTHER READING

Warder Clyde Allee. *The Social Life of Animals.* New York: W. W. Norton and Company, 1938.

Whately Carington. *Thought Transference.* New York: Creative Age Press, 1946.

Kurt Lewin. *A Dynamic Theory of Personality.* New York: McGraw-Hill Book Company, 1935.

Kurt Lewin. *Resolving Social Conflicts.* (Michigan University Research Center for Group Dynamics Publications.) New York: Harper and Brothers, 1946.

Gardner Murphy. *Parapsychology.* Encyclopaedia of Psychology, Edited by Philip Lawrence Harriman. New York: Philosophical Library, 1946.

J. G. Pratt and Others. *Extra-Sensory Perception After Sixty Years.* New York: Henry Holt and Company, 1940.

G. N. M. Tyrrell. *Science and Psychical Phenomena.* New York: Harper and Brothers, 1939.

Dr. Gardner Murphy is professor of psychology at The City College of New York. He is a member of the American Association for the Advancement of Science and the American Psychological Association, of which he was president 1943-4. He was 1932 winner of the Butler

Medal of Columbia. His numerous writings include Experimental Social Psychology *(with L. B. Murphy and T. M. Newcomb),* General Psychology, Public Opinion and the Individual *(with R. Likert) and* Personality. *He was editor of* Outline of Abnormal Psychology, *1929, and* Human Nature and Enduring Peace, *1945.*

10

Philosophy and the Development of the World Man

CORNELIUS KRUSÉ

PHILOSOPHY, from its earliest appearance, has been interested in the problem of achieving a knowledge of self. It is well known that over the Delphic Oracle there were inscribed two great admonitions: "Nothing too much" and "Know thyself." This knowledge of self certainly always involved a knowledge of man's fellows. In spite of all the intervening centuries in which men have addressed themselves to the problem of coming to know the nature of man, much remains still to be done, especially with reference to the problem before us—how it is possible for contemporary man to become a citizen of the world with a sense of world solidarity. I am mindful, of course, that you have already heard spokesmen for the natural sciences, the social sciences, psychology, art, and religion in this series on the nature of man. Philosophy's approach is therefore only one among the foregoing many in the undertaking which The Church Peace Union has set before itself. But our specific problem is: What has philosophy to offer in developing a world outlook and in developing the world man?

First of all, we must look at the question of what philosophy is. Many definitions, of course, have been offered in the past, and not any of them seems completely satisfactory. But I understand that Carl Sandburg once collected at least

73

a hundred definitions of poetry. After all, it ought not to be too difficult to say, in a general way, what philosophy is and what it tries to do and what it could offer toward contributing to world understanding. In the first place, I think it may be said that philosophy is one of the great human enterprises along with science, art, and religion. It represents, along with these great human concerns, intrinsic values as contrasted with instrumental values. Along with the other three intrinsic values, it indicates what really makes life worth living. A possible definition might be that philosophy is the determined and systematic attempt to find the most comprehensive and best-tested answers to questions about the nature of the universe and man's place in it, answers that would satisfy both head and heart.

CONTEMPORARY INTEREST IN PHILOSOPHY

We are living at a time when, in spite of engrossment in material things, there is much interest in philosophy. A few years ago the American Philosophical Association under a grant from the Rockefeller Foundation appointed a commission whose task was to see how the values of philosophy could be made more generally available in education in our country. The commission studied this problem for about a year and a half and organized many regional conferences in strategic places in this country. Those participating in the study were agreeably surprised to see the interest and challenge that were brought to the conference by professional people and representatives of the public at large who were not professional philosophers. They became convinced that we are living in a time when high expectations confront philosophy if philosophers will only address themselves to the great problems confronting mankind, and will speak in a language that can be more generally understood.

It is also true that the new cultural organization that has grown out of the United Nations, namely, Unesco, is likewise expecting much from philosophy and the humanities in general. A year or so ago the National Commission of Unesco in its annual meeting addressed itself to this question: What kind of understanding is it that we need in order to achieve what Unesco so ardently desires to work for, namely, peace through understanding? Much was made of the fact that while there is almost universal agreement that world government of some sort can alone remove the threat of war, unfortunately there was, the world over, not yet formed the necessary sense of world community. The understanding that is needed is not simply the amassing of a great deal of information about cultures other than our own. It is possible to have much information and relatively little understanding. Understanding of the type that is required demands a sympathetic appreciation of the fundamental beliefs and values of any given culture. In short, the attainment of such understanding deeply involves the entire problem of value.

THE UNIVERSALITY OF MAN'S GREAT VALUES

One of the difficulties in the past has been the easy assumption that values represent simply the idiosyncrasies of any given person or people, that values are matters of taste about which proverbially there should be no discussion. Close examination, however, of the nature of values discloses the superficiality of this attitude. Certainly truth, beauty and goodness, though they may have many varying interpretations, are not in themselves simply expressions of subjective feelings. Value-skepticism is as demoralizing as skepticism in truth-seeking. The existence of error does not invalidate the validity of the search for truth. Similarly, diversity of judgments of value in the social sphere does not invalidate the quest for values that may be and ought to be universally shared. In any case, far too much has been made of diversity and too little attention has been paid to great areas of agreement which already are established. Justice and friendship are certainly not simply Western ideals, nor those peculiar to any one given country. Under the impact of the war, it was shown how defenseless democracy is if it is simply what happens to be an American prejudice and not a universal value.

It is heartening to see that, at least in American philosophical thinking, there has been a great advance in the last twenty or twenty-five years in the direction of the recognition of the objectivity and consequent universality of some of man's great values. If philosophy is going to have any contribution to make to the formation of the world man, if it is to prepare him for participation in the world community, philosophy must show, and does, how he can free himself from particularistic involvements. We must seek universal values which may unite all mankind.

Such a search for universal values does not in the slightest involve the uncritical acceptance of any proposed value as deserving of universal acclaim. Once more Socrates' conviction that the unexamined life is not worth living would have to be brought to bear upon this problem. The values proposed for universal assent would really have to persuade mankind as a whole.

Furthermore, the search for universal values does not in the slightest mean a denial of the existence of special values or a rejection of diversity in values. Even the same fundamental values might receive many variant expressions. Orchestrated unity rather than the unity of unrelieved homogeneity is what is desired.

THE LANGUAGE BARRIER

Granted that men of good will are eager to acknowledge the possibility of universal values, and are ready to engage upon a search for them, making full allowance for the variety that would give unity in difference, how further shall we proceed?

Aristotle once said wisely that the will to friendship is a matter of a moment, but not friendship. Much effort will be

required for the modern man to come to know sympathetically cultures other than his own.

There is, in the first place, a great language barrier. The
learning of languages is a necessary but not a sufficient condition for providing modern man with the understanding
that is wanted. But the removal of the language barrier is
an inescapable prerequisite. Not all of us can learn all of
the languages of the world, but some of us will have to learn
some of them. No man of good will in our day should be anything less than bilingual. The time has passed for Americans
to take the attitude that if any language is to be learned by
anyone, it must always be English. Millions of Russians are
learning English; but not fifty thousand Americans are en-
gaged in the learning of Russian, at least in our universities
and colleges.

UNDERSTANDING OTHER PEOPLES AND CULTURES

Languages, of course, are only a key. Frequently transla-
tions must suffice. But in any case we must sympathetically
attempt to enter into the innermost dwelling-place of what
makes life seem worth living to people in cultures other than
our own. To know the art, the philosophy, and the religion
of other peoples is to come close to understanding from the
inside what constitutes the deeper reason for their mode of
behavior.

Much is made in our day of iron curtains, and they unfortunately exist. But most of the iron curtains are in our own
minds and are of our own devising—curtains of ignorance,
pride, indolence and fear. There have been no iron curtains
for us in China or India; and yet how many of us have sufficient knowledge of the cultures of these countries to enter
sympathetically into their innermost values? Russia no doubt
will be one day as open as her great plains. How many of us
are preparing now to avail ourselves of this opportunity
when and if it comes?

Universities and students have a very great new burden

placed upon them in order to be adequately prepared for the demands of the new day, demands which cannot be postponed. One of the great heresies of our day is the policy of perpetual postponement, under a sense of urgency, of the things that most urgently need doing. It takes time for trees to grow. If one is inhibited from planting them because fruit cannot be instantly gathered, there will never be fruit.

Admittedly, philosophy's contribution to world understanding cannot be given overnight, but it is of the first importance. Perpetual rejection of its contribution would be a great disaster in the long run. Acceptance of it might still make it possible for mankind to realize, in the words of a Greek poet, how amiable is man when he is really man.

SUGGESTIONS FOR FURTHER READING

Surendranath Dasgupta. *History of Indian Philosophy*. Cambridge: University Press, 1922.

William Ernest Hocking. *Living Religions and a World Faith*. New York: The Macmillan Company, 1940.

K. S. Latourette. *The Chinese, Their History and Culture*. New York: The Macmillan Company, 1934.

Charles A. Moore, Editor. *Philosophy; East and West*. Princeton: Princeton University Press, 1944.

Charles Morris. *Paths of Life*. New York: Harper and Brothers, 1942.

F. S. C. Northrop. *The Meeting of East and West*. New York: The Macmillan Company, 1946.

Kenneth James Saunders. *The Ideals of East and West*. New York: The Macmillan Company, 1934.

Krishnalal Shridharani. *My India, My America*. New York: Duell, Sloan and Pearce, 1941.

Dr. Cornelius Krusé has been chairman of the Department of Philosophy at Wesleyan University since 1930. His non-teaching activities include chairmanship of the First Inter-American Congress of

Philosophy, membership on a cultural mission to Latin America under auspices of the Coordinator's Office for Inter-American Affairs, official North American delegate to and vice president of the Congrès International de Philosophie *at Port au Prince, Haiti. He has been active in the American Friends Service Committee,* Société Franco-Americaine de Philosophie, *and the American Philosophical Association, of which he is a past president. He has contributed to philosophical journals and is co-author of* The Nature of Religious Experience, Essays in Honor of Douglas Clyde MacIntosh. *He is chairman of the American Council of Learned Societies. He was a member of the East-West Philosophers' Conference, held during June 20-July 29, 1949 in Honolulu, Hawaii.*

11

Summary and Synthesis

LEWIS MUMFORD

ALL OVER the world men are inquiring with fresh zeal into the nature of man, and the question naturally arises as to why we are so concerned at present with this topic. One explanation would be that man, during the last few centuries, has misinterpreted his own nature and has not, therefore, made the best of his possibilities. In reaction against an archaic theological view which exaggerated the significance, if not the powers, of the individual, we have, in the development of science, treated man as if the differences that set him off from his animal ancestors and co-partners were trivial ones. Primitive peoples made the error of treating things as· if they were persons, whereas modern man has made the equally fatal mistake of treating persons as if they were things. Modern man's conquest of nature has resulted in the displacement of man and, as a result, western civilization shows many evidences of social and personal disintegration.

THE NIHILISM OF A MECHANISTIC VIEW

Although many of the elements in man's nature remain constant, such as the need of air, water and food, his nature as a whole is being steadily modified, from place to place and era to era, by his culture. Our present conception of man is mainly the product of the mechanical and scientific culture that grew up at the end of the sixteenth century in western Europe. This culture, reacting against the subjective disorder that followed the breakup of the Middle Ages, sought to impose an arbitrary order and continuity by turning its back on the inner world; it rejected the subjective and autonomous aspects of personality and confined its attention to the external world: the world of the measurable, the repeatable, the standardizable. Emotion and feeling, quality and value, plan and purpose, the very sources of man's humanness, were looked upon, in this mechanistic mythology, as subjective and, therefore, unreal. This view rejected man's whole nature and lost sight of the larger whole in which human culture itself operates. Modern man has tried to understand the whole in terms of the unrelated parts; he has explained the higher aspects of culture and personality solely on the basis of lower processes which have not as yet reached the same degree of maturity and complexity; he has pushed back his inquiries into origins and lost sight of man's destinations. What was called, by definition, the real world was a world without value, significance or purpose.

Only now are we beginning to understand the ultimate nihilism and practical destructiveness of this limited view of man and his destiny. Those who are still immersed in this mechanical ideology produce as their ideal personality Superman and other mechanical comic strip heroes, creatures who, endowed with the latest instruments of physical science, travel by means of rockets and space-ships but live in a moral jungle more hostile to human development than the most primeval environment. The Nazis who systematically exterminated, with every refinement of torture, from six to seven million innocent human beings are matched by the active native psychopaths who, unconscious of the moral degradation involved, are planning even greater orgies of atomic or bacterial annihilation. It is evident that unless modern man understands the latent forces of creativity and renewal, he will become the victim of the very machines on which he overconcentrated his attention.

THE MODERN SCIENTIFIC VIEW OF MAN

Now what does modern science tell us about the nature of man? Already we know a great deal that was not included in the seventeenth century analysis of matter and motion. We find that a tendency toward organization and development seems to have been active even in the purely physical universe before life itself appeared. The bio-chemist, L. J. Henderson, has pointed out the peculiar conditions of our special planet which predisposed it for that manifestation which we regard as life. Wherever we look, interdependence, mutual aid and dynamic balance are conditions for the further activities of growth and development. The emergent characteristics of life—self-direction, purposiveness, sensitivity and selectivity—reach a culmination in man, who is able to turn nature to his own special uses and create, for his further growth, a world of forms, values and meanings, communicable and sharable, which greatly increase his range in time and space.

But man has a social nature as well as a biological one. Society was invented hundreds of millions of years ago by insects like the ants. But man escaped the stabilities and automatisms of animal society by contriving a super-organic culture by means of which he could experimentally transform his own nature without fixing those changes irretrievably into his own bodily organs. Neither man's world nor his self is ready made. Through language man has projected his feelings and emotions and has created a common store of shared meanings; he has, by manual skill and ingenuity, reshaped his environment and made it more habitable; and by dream and wish and ideal, he has added another dimension to his existence—the future—and now lives no small part of his life by anticipation. In short, man is a self-fabricating. animal in an unfinished world. His nature is incomplete and self-transcending, and the most careful description of it remains inadequate because it will not be revealed in its fullness till "the end of history."

MAN'S IMPULSE TO SELF-PERFECTION

The scientific description of man has given us invaluable insights into human nature. But such analysis is incomplete because it deals exclusively with the past, has no place for potentiality and purpose and is confined to repetitions and statistical probabilities. It has no understanding of what is creative, emergent and unique and, therefore, it overlooks the very deep tendency that religion has hitherto constantly emphasized—man's impulse to self-perfection. To describe man without taking into account his capacity to discriminate, to evaluate, to select and to control, is to overlook the most characteristic elements in his nature. Much of modern man's debasement and self-contempt is due to the fact that our scientific interpretations tend to reduce higher functions to lower ones, thereby nullifying all of man's dearly won distinctions and achievements: self-consciousness, self-direction and self-renewal.

Albert Schweitzer, after the first World War, diagnosed the present crisis in civilization and said that it was due to our failure to create a life-affirming ethics. When I first read that statement, it seemed to me to be over-simplified; but further observation and reflection have convinced me that Schweitzer touched the core of our difficulties. Man's continued development which alone can save him from arrest or regression depends upon a threefold process of evaluation and, unless he knows what is good and bad for him, man's concepts as to what is false or true will be partial and erroneous.

THREE KINDS OF EVALUATION

The first of the three kinds of evaluation is quantitative: a matter of more or less. The Confucian and the Aristotelian doctrines of the Golden Mean do justice to this aspect of man's development. Our age is proudly quantity-minded; and yet both piety and cynicism have, from quite different motives, overlooked the way in which quantities alter qualities. The control of quantity is one of the prime steps in ethical development.

The second kind is qualitative: a choice of higher and lower. All organic needs exist in a hierarchic order. The lower needs, like breathing and drinking, though absolutely essential to life, are valuable only if subordinate to feeling and thinking. What value would a hundred years of life have, for example, if one were compelled to spend all of it in an iron lung? Human life is a constant push upward from conditioned and automatic activities to released and creative ones. Unfortunately, in our present civilization, the higher functions are made subservient to the lower ones; art becomes a means of selling goods, and language, debased by newspapers and radio, becomes a dingy medium of publicity and advertisement.

The third process of evaluation has to do with purpose. There can be no adequate concept of good without cosmic perspective, this leading to the understanding of a final good beyond that of the immediate personality or the immediate community. In all life-sustaining activities, one needs the right quantity of the right quality, in the right order, for the right end. The good is the life-furthering, the integrating, the purposeful, the significant; while the bad is another name for the life-defeating, the disintegrating, the purposeless, the insignificant or nihilistic.

Once we fully understand that man's nature is incomplete and self-transcending, we shall feel free once more to ask what kind of man, what kind of society, we must create in order to overcome our present disintegration and, thereby, effect the passage from the closed societies of the past to the open society, the world community, which is the final goal that has become visible in our time.

REQUIREMENTS FOR THE LIFE-AFFIRMING SELF

Modern man must create a new self more consonant with his actual nature and his potentialities than that which our present culture has produced; he must develop a self capable of planning and creating a more unified world which will do justice to all of his capacities and which will control the life-defeating processes that are now at work. Some of the requirements for this new self, if we are to overcome the "crisis of our age," are:

1. *Balance.* The fullest possible use of every aptitude within an orderly pattern of continued growth. This implies breaking with the mechanistic conception of the fragmentary over-specialized man, the "reversed cripple" of Nietzsche, a giant in one function and a dwarf in every other.

2. *Inhibition.* The greater the powers of nature that man commands, the greater the need for effective control. All of man's higher activities depend upon the exertion of a greater degree of conscious direction. Our powers of inhibition must be proportionate to our powers of expression.

3. *Sacrifice.* In order to achieve balance, we must, as Dr. C. G. Jung counsels, favor our weak side and weaken our strong side. An extroverted age must turn inward; a materialistic age must cultivate spirit; a mechanistic culture must nourish the spontaneous and the unique: all to the end that every aspect of man's essential nature shall be represented and fully utilized in both the persons and the community.

THE ROLE OF PERSONALITY IN WORLD COMMUNITY

What is the test of this new self? First we must ask, do our acts tend to produce that type of person who is able to transcend the limits of closed groups while, at the same time, helping to reduce their resultant hostility, aggression and defensive enclosure. Do we overcome the isolation of class, rank, party, nationality and creed? Do we give ourselves to expanding the area of communication and communion, of mutual aid and love, to the end that we shall, in time, produce a world community? Each group must consciously take part in this change from closed to open societies. Do we arrange our daily functions in the order of their true importance for human development or are we the automatic victims of external pressures and irrelevant claims? Without a discipline for the daily life which will modify every activity in the direction of autonomy and purposefulness and freedom, we shall probably lack the strength to conquer the disintegrating elements in our society.

Actually, the role of personality is a decisive one in the present crisis. Only the fuller understanding of man's whole · nature, in the dimensions revealed by religion and philosophy as well as those described by the sciences, will help modern man to create a new self which will redeem him from the repetitive world of mechanism and the meaningless world of nihilism. Modern man needs that self-knowledge to give him the energy and faith to create a culture in which power and intelligence will, for all men, become the willing servants of love.

SUGGESTIONS FOR FURTHER READING

Henry Adams. *The Degradation of the Democratic Dogma*. New York: The Macmillan Company, 1919.

Henri Bergson. *The Two Sources of Morality and Religion*. New York: Henry Holt and Company, 1935.

Jakob Burckhardt. *Force and Freedom; Reflections on History*. New York: Pantheon Books, Inc., 1943.

Charles Morris. *Paths of Life; Preface to a World Religion*. New York: Harper and Brothers, 1942.

Arnold Toynbee. *A Study of History*. 6 Volumes. London: Oxford University Press, 1934-1939.

Mr. Lewis Mumford has been visiting professor at Dartmouth College and The University of North Carolina, professor of Humanities at Stan-

ford University and Earl lecturer, Pacific School of Religion. He was awarded the Townsend Harris Medal, 1939, Howard Memorial Medal, 1946 and Guggenheim fellowships in 1932 and 1938. He is a fellow of the American Academy of Arts and Sciences. His writings include: Herman Melville, Technics and Civilization, Faith for Living, The Culture of Cities, *and* The Condition of Man.

Appendix

APPENDIX A

Selected Bibliography

IN ADDITION to the books listed at the end of each chapter, the following works are directly related to the subject matter of this symposium.

Swami Akhilanandi. *The Hindu View of Christ.* New York: Philosophical Library, 1949.

Robert O. Ballou in collaboration with Friedrich Spiegelberg and with the assistance and advice of Horace L. Friess, ed. *The Bible of the World.* New York: Viking Press, 1938.

L. Adams Beck. *The Story of Oriental Philosophy.* New York: Cosmopolitan Book Corporation, 1928.

Theos Bernard. *Hindu Philosophy.* New York: Philosophical Library, 1947.

A. Cohen. *Everyman's Talmud.* New York: E. P. Dutton and Company, 1949.

H. G. Creel. *Confucius: The Man and the Myth.* New York: The John Day Company, 1949.

Kedarnath Das Gupta. *Essence of Religion.* New York: World Fellowship of Faiths, 1941.

Christopher Dawson. *Religion and Culture.* New York: Sheed and Ward, 1948.

Vergilius Ferm, ed. *Forgotten Religions.* New York: Philosophical Library, 1950.

Theodore Meyer Greene. *The Arts and the Art of Criticism.* Princeton University Press, 1940.

E. R. Hughes, ed. and trans. *Chinese Philosophy in Classical Times.* New York: E. P. Dutton and Company, 1942.

Hans Kohn. *The Twentieth Century.* New York: The Macmillan Company, 1949.

91

E. G. Lee. *Mass Man and Religion*. New York: Harper and Brothers. 1948.

Jacques Maritain. *True Humanism*. New York: Charles Scribner's and Sons, 1938.

Wong Mou-Lam, trans. *The Sutra of Wei Lang*. London: Luzac and Company, 1947.

Reinhold Niebuhr. *The Nature and Destiny of Man*, Vol. I, *Human Nature*, 1941; Vol. II, *Human Destiny*, 1943. New York: Charles Scribner's and Sons.

John B. Noss. *Man's Religions*. New York: The Macmillan Company, 1949.

H. A. Overstreet *The Mature Mind*. New York: W. W. Norton and Company, 1949.

Marco Palis. *Peaks and Lamas*. New York: Alfred A. Knopf, 1949. (Revised Edition.)

E. H. Palmer, trans. *The Koran (Qur'an)*. New York: Oxford University Press, 1928.

Bertrand Russell. *Authority and the Individual*. New York: Simon and Schuster, 1949.

Albert Schweitzer. *The Philosophy of Civilization*. New York: The Macmillan Company, 1949.

Laurence Stapleton. *The Design of Democracy*. New York: Oxford University Press, 1949.

Milton Steinberg. *Basic Judaism*. New York: Harcourt Brace and Company, 1947.

Hugh C. Stuntz. *The United Nations Challenge to the Church*. New York: Abingdon-Cokesbury Press, 1948.

Jungiro Takakusa. *The Essentials of Buddhist Philosophy*. Honolulu: University of Hawaii, 1947.

Arthur Waley. *The Way and Its Power*. London: George Allen and Unwin, 1934.

Daniel Day Williams. *God's Grace and Man's Hope*. New York: Harper and Brothers, 1949.

Lin Yutang, ed. *The Wisdom of China and India. An Anthology*. New York: Random House, 1942.

Suggestions for Arranging a Seminar on the Nature of Man

A PRIMARY reason for the publication of this book is the hope that other communities across the land will arrange series of discussion groups on the nature of man.

Those who have read this book will realize that a study of human nature is not an academic pastime in our day. We have seen that leaders of thought trace the so-called "crisis of our civilization" to a crisis in man himself. Hence they tell us that if we would understand our age with its problems of crucial importance, we must find a deeper insight into the nature of man. For modern man, responsible for the emergence of most of the problems which he faces, must assume responsibility for finding a workable solution to them.

The following suggestions may prove useful to community leaders who wish to arrange a seminar on the nature of man.

SPONSORING ORGANIZATIONS

A community-wide program is always most effective. Therefore, it is well to enlist as sponsors for a series of meetings as many different types of organizations as possible. For instance, churches, synagogues, service clubs, world affairs and United Nations groups, women's groups, young people's groups and other volunteer organizations—all these should be represented among the sponsors. A joint committee should be named to have overall charge of arrangements.

SPEAKERS

Many communities could arrange a series on the nature of man by using its own leaders in the schools, professional fields and business world. These leaders could serve as speakers, chairmen, discussion leaders. Speakers should be picked not only for their knowledge of the subject but for their ability to present it understandingly to an audience. The chairman for each meeting should also be selected with care; for in addition to being able to lead discussion, he should have enough background of the topic to be discussed so that he can, if necessary, assist the speaker in analyzing or answering questions.

DIVERSE REPRESENTATION AMONG PARTICIPANTS

An effort should be made to have many nationalities, races, and religious groups represented in the program. In the New York series, representatives from different denominations and faiths offered the invocation at the various meetings. Students from other lands can often make a special contribution to a program of this kind. They can frequently be found at nearby colleges, and they are usually glad to cooperate in a program that aims to develop more world understanding.

PROMOTION

The entire series as well as each meeting must be given wide publicity. Newspaper editors will usually cooperate by printing news stories, pictures, and, on occasion, editorials. Letters to the editor can also be used effectively to draw attention to the series. If some funds are available to cover printing costs, programs and attractive posters should be widely used. The posters can be placed on bulletin boards in public buildings, churches, colleges and, at times, can also be used in stores. Programs can be circulated directly or through the mails among the sponsoring organizations and any other community groups which might be interested.

Actually, the cooperating community organizations can do the most valuable work in rallying the people of the area to attend the meetings.

Perhaps the most effective way to stimulate the attendance is by use of the telephone. Excellent results have been obtained by organizing teams of men, women, and young people to telephone to individuals to whom programs have already been sent. The telephone call serves not only as a means to personalize the invitation, but also is a reminder of the printed material sent through the mails. In some communities a second telephone call has been used with gratifying success.

Arrangements can often be made with the local radio stations for spot announcements. It may also be possible to arrange for programs on the radio—brief addresses by guest speakers or round table discussions on several of the subjects of the series.

SIZE OF MEETINGS

Large Discussion Meeting. For the large meeting it probably will be necessary to invite a guest speaker to give an address on the subject. At least half of the available time should be devoted to audience participation. (In the New York series, audiences varied from 200 to 350. Each 45-minute address was followed by a 45-minute discussion period. Animated discussions revealed the live interest of contemporary people in the subject matter of this series.) If discussion is not to prove rambling and aimless, a large responsibility falls on the discussion leader. Not only must he guide the discussion and keep it close to the subject, but he must be able at the conclusion of the meeting to give a brief, cogent summary of the points developed in the discussion.

Small Discussion Group. A series on the nature of man might be planned for a small discussion group with 15 to 18 members. In such a group this book might be used as a discussion guide. The suggestions for further reading listed at the end of each chapter would provide participants with an opportunity to study the subject in advance of the actual meeting.

The small discussion group, taken in a unique sense, is a democratic device. Democracy evolves from the process of "talking things over," for the discussion group offers each participant an opportunity to express and clarify his ideas. Such meetings may be arranged in churches, synagogues, or other voluntary organizations. The neighborhood meeting in a private home can be especially significant and helpful.

GUIDES ON TECHNIQUES

Various books and pamphlets on techniques are available to give helpful advice. The following should be especially useful:

Here's How It's Done by Florence Widutis. New York: Post War Information Exchange, 1945.

Education for Maturity by John Walker Powell. New York: Hermitage House, Inc., 1949. An essay on adult group study.

How to Make Friends for Your Church by John L. Fortson. New York: Association Press, 1943.

Kansas Story on Unesco. Department of State Publication 3378. International Organization & Conference Series IV. United Nations Educational, Scientific & Cultural Organization 7. A step-by-step description of how a state council for Unesco was organized and is now contributing to international understanding and peace.

The Background of the Lecture Series on *The Nature of Man*

THIS SERIES of lectures on *The Nature of Man* has a history that may interest the general reader. Therefore the following background data are presented in some detail:

WORLD FAITHS ROUND TABLE

During the summer of 1946, the Town Hall in New York City conducted a ten-week World Faiths Round Table in an endeavor to stimulate a closer unity and better understanding among the peoples of the world. Dr. George V. Denny, Jr., President of Town Hall, Mrs. Ruth Cranston, a life-long student of world religions, and Mrs. Clair Courteol Deane, an indefatigable worker for peace, were in charge of the project. Under their leadership, the basic teachings and ideals of the outstanding world faiths were discussed and ten basic principles, acceptable to all faiths, were agreed upon, these constituting a basis for discussion.

These ten points taught by all faiths are:

1. The unity of life.
2. The interdependence and brotherhood of all men.
3. Love and service to fellow-man: not domination and attempted power over him.
4. Non-violence and non-injury: no more war or killing.
5. Help—not exploitation—of the weak and backward.
6. Purity—and personal disinterestedness.
7. True riches and true happiness are within. The object of life is not a mad race for the accumulation of money and material things. The true kingdom of heaven is within you. The goal of life is the fullest development of man's

highest powers—mental, moral and spiritual.

8. The worth of individual man and the ability of every man to attain states of life far above those he is now experiencing. Discipline and purity of life are necessary for this attainment: the leaving of a lesser life to gain a greater.
9. The immortality of the soul—and ultimately:
10. The union of man with God: the final truth of every religion.

During the ten-week period of the World Faiths Round Table, constructive contributions to the work of the United Nations were achieved and, due to national newspaper publicity, requests from clubs, church groups, schools and colleges for permission to incorporate a World Faith study scheme into their own work came from all parts of the country.

At a final meeting, open to the general public, on Sunday evening, September 8, 1946, in the Town Hall Auditorium, representatives of many religions gave addresses; among the leaders were Swami Nikhilananda, Dr. Lin Yutang, Dr. Taraknath Das, Dr. S. H. Goldenson, Mrs. Beraet Enata, and Dr. Joseph R. Sizoo. The United Nations was represented by Dr. Lena Madesin Phillips, who spoke on "The United Nations and World Faith." Three main topics which concerned continued work toward international religious understanding and tolerance were outlined:

1. Research in relation to the basic principles of the religions of the world, with supplementary studies on the lives of the respective founders.
2. Applications of the ten basic religious principles to practical affairs, that is, how such principles can work with or apply to governmental, economic, social and racial problems, etc. Such research, it was realized, would entail a resumé of the concrete achievements in international relations up to the time of the establishment of the United Nations.
3. A study of the nature of man. This would be an analysis of the human mind and spirit in the light of recent scientific discoveries, with particular emphasis placed on those tech-

niques which would lead to better understanding and control of "our inner instrument."

CONFERENCE OF RELIGION

A Conference of Religion for Moral and Spiritual Support
of the United Nations was held at Town Hall in New York
City on June 16, 17, and 18, 1948. These meetings were
sponsored by The Church Peace Union, the American Association for the United Nations, and the World Alliance
for International Friendship through Religion, in cooperation with some fifty allied organizations.

The sessions were arranged under three headings: (1) The
United Nations and Its Task, (2) The Moral and Religious
Resources of Mankind, and (3) Religion and Human Rights.
Spokesmen representing many nations and the world's major
religions helped to make this conference a dynamic and co-
operative success. The conference speeches were published
under the title, *A Spiritual Approach to the Problems of
Peace.*

THE NATURE OF MAN

During the intervening period since 1946, the date of the
World Faiths Round Table, Mrs. Cranston, one of the direc-
tors of that project, had been working on the idea of a series
of lectures on the subject of *The Nature of Man.* She had
discussed the idea with leading authors, scholars and scientists throughout the country. Late in 1948, she presented her
completed plan to Dr. Henry A. Atkinson, General Secretary
of The Church Peace Union. *The Nature of Man* was to be
the theme for ten lectures which would be given by authori-
ties in the fields of the natural sciences, the social sciences,
art, religion, and philosophy. Dr. Atkinson felt that such a
series of addresses would not only be provocative but could
be a challenging and important presentation of facts about
human nature. Such a seminar, moreover, was in line with
the motivating ideals of The Church Peace Union to bring

about a unity in the midst of diverse viewpoints. The lecture
series accordingly was presented in the spring of 1949.

The Program of the New York Lecture Series

MAN'S PLACE IN NATURE AS SEEN BY A BIOLOGIST

Invocation—DR. JOHN HOWLAND LATHROP
  Minister, Church of the Saviour
  Brooklyn, New York

Chairman—DR. GEORGE V. DENNY, JR.
  President, Town Hall
  New York City

Speaker—DR. EDMUND W. SINNOTT

MAN AND THE EARTH THAT SUPPORTS HIM

Invocation—REV. IRA LANGSTON
  Minister, Park Avenue Christian Church
  New York City

Chairman—MRS. WILLIAM DICK SPORBORG
  Member of the United States Commission for Unesco
  Member of the Board of the American Association for the
  United Nations

Speaker—DR. KIRTLEY F. MATHER

THE SOCIAL SCIENCES

Invocation—DR. HARRY N. HOLMES
  Secretary of Interchange Committee on Speakers and
  Preachers

Chairman—DR. HARRY J. CARMAN
  Dean of Columbia College
  Columbia University, New York City

Speaker—DR. ORDWAY TEAD

PSYCHOLOGY AND PSYCHOTHERAPY

Invocation—Dr. Ladislas Harsanyi
First Magyar Presbyterian Church
New York City

Chairman—Dr. Horace Friess
Professor of Philosophy
Columbia University, New York City

Speaker—Dr. Brand Blanshard

ART AND THE NATURE OF MAN

Invocation—Rev. Jesse W. Stitt
Minister, Village Presbyterian Church
New York City

Chairman—Dr. Thomas Clark Pollock
Dean of the College of Arts and Sciences
New York University, New York City

Speaker—Dr. Theodore Greene

RELIGIOUS DISCIPLINES

Invocation—Rev. Thomas Sparks
Cathedral of St. John the Divine
New York City

Chairman—Dr. Walter D. Head
President, World Alliance for International Friendship
Through Religion, New York City

Speakers—Rev. Dr. John Sutherland Bonnell

Dr. Taraknath Das

MAN AND HIS DESTINY

Invocation—Swami Aseshananda
Ramakrishna-Vivekananda Center
New York City

Chairman—Dr. Henry James Forman
Former editor of *Collier's* and Associate of the *North American Review*

Speaker—Dr. Gardner Murphy

PHILOSOPHY AND THE DEVELOPMENT OF THE WORLD MAN

Invocation—REV. ALEXANDER SIME
  Fifth Avenue Presbyterian Church
  New York City

Chairman—DR. CHARLES W. HENDEL
  Professor of Philosophy
  Yale University, New Haven, Conn.

Speaker—DR. CORNELIUS KRUSÉ

SUMMARY AND SYNTHESIS

Invocation—RABBI SIDNEY I. GOLDSTEIN
  Temple Sharey Tifilo
  East Orange, New Jersey

Chairman—DR. HENRY A. ATKINSON
  General Secretary, The Church Peace Union *and the* World
  Alliance for International Friendship Through Religion

Speaker—MR. LEWIS MUMFORD

Index

A

Aggression, 86
Agricultural resources, 14, 16ff., 24
Alcibiades, 55
Alcoholics Anonymous, 49
Allee, Warder C., 61
American Association for the United Nations, 99
Anthropology, 24
Aristotelian doctrine of Golden Mean, 84
Aristotle, 31, 32, 35, 76
Art, vi, 2, Ch. 6, 73, 74, 77, 85, 99
Atkinson, Henry A., viii, 99

B

Beauty, 2, 9, 26, 75
Beethoven, 8, 41
Behaviorism, 30
Bergson, Henri, 8
Bhagavad Gita, 54, 58
Biochemistry, 7
Biology, 8, 24
Biophysics, 7
Blanshard, Brand, vi, 29, 36
Bonnell, John S., vi, 47, 51
Braque, Georges, 39

C

Chase, Stuart, 24
Christian humanism, 2, 3ff.
Christian tradition, The, 29
Chrow, Lawrence, vii
Church, The, 51
Church Peace Union, The, vii, 73, 99

L

Lenin, 25
Lewin, Kurt, 67
Loos, A. William, vii
Lord's Prayer, The, 58
Love, 86, 87
"Love of man," 23, 25, 27
"Love of truth," 23, 27
Lucretius, 47

M

Malthusian principle, 20
Marx, Karl, 25
Materialism, 2, 10, 29ff., 51, 55
Mather, Kirtley F., vi, 13, 22
McDougall, William, 32
Mechanistic view of life, 2, 8, 82, 86
Medicine, 8, 24, 47
Menninger, Karl, 50
Middle Ages, 82
Millikan, Robert A., 48
Mind, 29, 30, 32
Mineral interdependence, 16, 21
Mineral resources, 13ff.
Morality, 9, 26
Mumford, Lewis, vii, 81, 87
Murphy, Gardner, vi, 61, 70
Mutual aid, 62, 83, 86
Mysticism, 9

N

Natural sciences, 24, 73, 99
Nature, 1, 3, 7, 9
Needham, Joseph, 9
New Testament, 3
Newton, Isaac, 67
Nietzsche, F. W., 86
Noyes, Jr., William A., 48

O

Old Testament, 3
Osborn, Henry F., 48

P

Painting, Ch. 6
Paul, Saint, 50, 69